Stress Management for Couples and Relationships

Copyright Page

TITLE: Stress Management for Couples and Relationships

1ST Edition

Copyright @ 2023

ISBN: 9798223045076

Table of Contents

Stress Management for Couples and Relationships

By Roberto Miguel Rodriguez

Book Outline

By focusing on stress management, "Love Under Pressure" empowers individuals and couples to navigate the complexities of modern life without sacrificing their relationships. Through practical techniques, insights, and real-life examples, this book serves as a valuable resource for anyone seeking to strengthen their relationship amidst the pressures of today's world.

Understanding and Managing Stress

In this chapter, we delve into the fundamentals of stress, exploring its causes, symptoms, and effects on both physical and mental health. Readers will gain valuable insights into their own stress triggers and learn effective techniques for managing stress in their daily lives.

Workplace Stress Management

For those struggling with work-related stress, this chapter offers practical tips and strategies for creating a healthy work-life balance, managing deadlines and expectations, and fostering positive relationships with colleagues.

Stress Management for Parents and Caregivers

Parenting and caregiving can be exhausting and overwhelming. This chapter provides guidance on how to navigate the challenges of raising children or caring for loved ones, while also prioritizing self-care and managing stress effectively.

Stress Management for Students and Academics

In the competitive world of academia, stress can be a constant companion. This chapter offers valuable techniques for managing exam anxiety, dealing with academic pressure, and achieving a healthy work-study-life balance.

Stress Management for Entrepreneurs and Business Owners

Running a business comes with its unique set of stressors. This chapter provides entrepreneurs and business owners with strategies for maintaining resilience, managing uncertainty, and preventing burnout while striving for success.

Stress Management for Athletes and Sports Professionals

Athletes and sports professionals face immense pressure to perform at their best. This chapter explores techniques for managing pre-competition nerves, dealing with high-pressure situations, and maintaining mental and physical well-being.

Stress Management for Healthcare Professionals

Healthcare professionals often face intense stress due to the demanding nature of their work. This chapter offers practical tools for coping with compassion fatigue, managing patient expectations, and prioritizing self-care in a challenging environment.

Stress Management for Veterans and Military Personnel

Military personnel and veterans often carry the burden of stress long after their service. This chapter addresses the unique challenges they face and provides strategies for managing post-traumatic stress, transitioning to civilian life, and building resilience.

Stress Management for Seniors and Retirees

In this chapter, we explore the stressors that come with aging and retirement. Readers will discover techniques for maintaining emotional well-being, staying socially connected, and embracing a fulfilling life during the golden years.

Stress Management for Individuals with Chronic Illnesses or Disabilities

Living with chronic illnesses or disabilities can be incredibly challenging. This chapter offers support and guidance for managing stress, finding emotional resilience, and adapting to a new normal.

Stress Management for Couples and Relationships

Finally, this chapter focuses on stress within relationships. Readers will learn effective communication techniques, conflict resolution strategies, and ways to support each other through stressful times, ultimately strengthening their bond.

Whether you're a parent, student, athlete, or entrepreneur, "Love Under Pressure" provides practical strategies and guidance for managing stress in various areas of life. This book aims to empower individuals and couples to navigate the modern world's stressors while fostering healthy relationships, personal well-being, and overall happiness.

Chapter 1: Understanding and Managing Stress

The Impact of Stress on Relationships

Stress is a common phenomenon experienced by individuals from all walks of life. It can stem from various sources such as work, family, finances, health, or personal obligations. While stress affects everyone differently, its impact on relationships is often profound and can have long-lasting consequences. In this subchapter, we will explore how stress can impact relationships and provide valuable insights on managing stress within couples and relationships.

Stress acts as a silent intruder, slowly seeping into the cracks of even the strongest relationships. It can lead to communication breakdowns, increased conflicts, and emotional disconnect between partners. As stress levels rise, individuals may become irritable, short-tempered, and less patient, which further strains the bond between couples. Moreover, the demands of everyday life combined with stress can leave little time and energy for nurturing the relationship, leading to feelings of neglect or detachment.

For individuals in the workplace, stress can spill over into their personal lives, affecting their ability to be present and engaged with their partners. Similarly, parents and caregivers face unique stressors that can impact their relationships, as the demands of raising children or taking care of aging parents can be overwhelming. Students and academics, entrepreneurs and business owners, athletes and sports professionals, healthcare professionals, veterans and military personnel, seniors and retirees, and individuals with chronic illnesses or disabilities – all face their own set of stressors that can strain their relationships.

However, understanding and managing stress within relationships is crucial for their survival and growth. This subchapter will provide practical strategies for couples to navigate through stressful periods, including effective communication techniques, stress reduction exercises, and tips for maintaining a healthy work-life balance. It will also delve into the importance of self-care and the role of empathy and support in strengthening relationships during times of stress.

By implementing these strategies, couples can not only weather the storm of stress but also emerge stronger and more connected. Love Under Pressure: Stress Management for Couples and Relationships in the Modern World aims to equip readers with the tools and knowledge to manage stress effectively, fostering healthier and happier relationships.

Whether you are a professional seeking stress management techniques or a couple looking to enhance your relationship amidst the pressures of life, this subchapter offers valuable insights and practical advice for understanding and managing stress within the intricate web of relationships. Prepare to embark on a transformative journey towards a stress-free and fulfilling love life.

Common Causes of Stress in Modern Relationships

In today's fast-paced and demanding world, stress has become a common feature in many relationships. Love Under Pressure: Stress Management for Couples and Relationships in the Modern World aims to shed light on the various factors that contribute to stress in relationships and offer effective strategies for managing it.

1. Communication Issues: Poor communication is one of the leading causes of stress in modern relationships. Misunderstandings, lack of effective communication skills, and not feeling heard or understood can result in frustration, tension, and conflict.

2. Work-Life Balance: The demands of modern life often make it challenging to strike a balance between work and personal life. Long work hours, constant connectivity, and the pressure to succeed can place a significant strain on relationships, leaving partners feeling neglected and stressed.

3. Financial Pressures: Financial stress is another common cause of strain in relationships. Managing finances, paying bills, and maintaining a certain lifestyle can lead to arguments, resentment, and anxiety about the future.

4. Parenting and Caregiving Responsibilities: Parents and caregivers often experience high levels of stress due to the demands of raising children, caring for aging parents, or supporting a loved one with special needs. Juggling these responsibilities while maintaining a healthy relationship can be overwhelming.

5. Academic and Career Pressure: Students, academics, entrepreneurs, athletes, healthcare professionals, and business owners face unique stressors related to their respective fields. Balancing academic or professional aspirations with relationship commitments can create tension and anxiety.

6. Past Trauma and Emotional Baggage: Individuals carrying unresolved past traumas or emotional baggage may struggle to maintain healthy relationships. The emotional weight of these experiences can lead to conflicts, trust issues, and difficulty in forming deep connections.

7. Health Challenges: Chronic illnesses, disabilities, or mental health conditions can significantly impact relationships. Coping with the physical and emotional toll of these challenges can strain even the strongest partnerships.

8. Aging and Life Transitions: Seniors, retirees, and individuals going through major life transitions such as retirement or empty nesting may experience stress as they navigate unfamiliar territory. Adjusting to new roles and routines can place strain on a relationship.

By understanding the common causes of stress in modern relationships, individuals can take proactive steps to manage and alleviate these stressors. Love Under Pressure offers practical advice, tools, and techniques to help couples and individuals navigate the complexities of modern life and build resilient, fulfilling relationships even in the face of stress.

Recognizing the Signs and Symptoms of Stress

Stress is an inevitable part of life, affecting people from all walks of life. From students to athletes, parents to entrepreneurs, and healthcare professionals to seniors, stress can impact anyone. In order to effectively manage stress, it is essential to first recognize its signs and symptoms. This subchapter aims to provide a comprehensive understanding of the various indicators of stress for individuals, couples, and relationships.

One of the most common physical signs of stress is fatigue. If you constantly feel tired, even after a good night's sleep, it may be a sign that stress is taking a toll on your body. Additionally, stress can manifest as headaches, muscle tension, and an increased susceptibility to illnesses. It is important to pay attention to these physical symptoms and take steps to address the underlying stressors.

Emotional and behavioral changes are also key indicators of stress. Excessive worrying, irritability, and mood swings may all be signs that stress is affecting your emotional well-being. Furthermore, changes in appetite, sleep patterns, and social interactions can be red flags for stress-related issues. Recognizing these changes and seeking support is crucial for maintaining overall mental health.

In relationships, stress can have a significant impact. Couples may experience increased arguments, lack of intimacy, or a feeling of disconnection when stress levels are high. Recognizing these signs early on can help couples address the underlying stressors and work together to find healthy coping mechanisms.

Understanding and managing stress in the workplace is vital for both employees and employers. Burnout, decreased productivity, and increased absenteeism may indicate that stress levels are reaching an unhealthy level. Identifying these signs can help individuals and organizations implement appropriate stress management strategies, such as promoting work-life balance and offering stress reduction programs.

Parents, caregivers, and students often face unique stressors. Recognizing signs such as difficulty concentrating, changes in behavior, or a decline in academic performance can be crucial in providing the support needed. Implementing stress management techniques, such as time management and self-care practices, can help individuals in these roles better cope with their stressors.

Entrepreneurs, athletes, healthcare professionals, veterans, seniors, and individuals with chronic illnesses or disabilities also face specific stressors. By recognizing signs such as increased anxiety, decreased motivation, or feelings of overwhelm, individuals can seek appropriate resources and support to manage stress effectively.

In conclusion, recognizing the signs and symptoms of stress is the first step towards effective stress management. Whether you are a student, caregiver, athlete, or entrepreneur, understanding the physical, emotional, and behavioral indicators of stress can help you take proactive steps to reduce its impact. By addressing stress early on, individuals, couples, and relationships can thrive in the modern world, creating a healthier and more fulfilling life.

The Connection Between Stress and Mental Health

Stress is a part of everyday life, and it affects each and every one of us at some point. However, what many people fail to realize is the profound impact stress can have on our mental health. In this subchapter, we will explore the intricate connection between stress and mental health, providing valuable insights and practical strategies for managing stress in various aspects of life.

Understanding and Managing Stress:

Stress is known to trigger a wide range of mental health issues, including anxiety, depression, and even more severe conditions like post-traumatic stress disorder (PTSD). We will delve into the scientific explanations behind this connection and help you understand the biological and psychological mechanisms at play. By gaining this understanding, you will be better equipped to recognize the signs of stress in yourself and others, and take proactive steps to manage it effectively.

Workplace Stress Management:

Many individuals find the workplace to be a significant source of stress. Whether it's the pressure to meet deadlines, navigate office politics, or achieve work-life balance, stress can take a toll on mental health. We will provide practical tips for managing workplace stress, such as setting boundaries, practicing self-care, and utilizing stress reduction techniques during breaks.

Stress Management for Parents and Caregivers:

Raising children or caring for dependents can be incredibly rewarding, but it also comes with its fair share of stressors. From juggling responsibilities to dealing with sleepless nights and challenging behaviors, parents and caregivers often find themselves overwhelmed.

We will explore strategies for managing parental stress, including seeking support, practicing self-compassion, and finding healthy outlets for stress relief.

Stress Management for Students and Academics:

Students and academics face unique stressors, including academic pressure, exams, and the constant pursuit of success. We will discuss effective stress management techniques tailored specifically for this audience, such as time management skills, mindfulness practices, and seeking academic support.

Stress Management for Entrepreneurs and Business Owners:

Running a business or being an entrepreneur can be highly rewarding, but it also comes with significant stress. We will delve into the specific challenges faced by entrepreneurs and offer strategies for managing stress in the fast-paced, high-pressure world of business. From setting realistic goals to maintaining work-life balance, we will explore practical solutions to help entrepreneurs thrive.

Stress Management for Athletes and Sports Professionals:

The world of sports can be physically and mentally demanding, with athletes and sports professionals constantly facing high-pressure situations. We will explore techniques for managing stress in the sports arena, including visualization exercises, relaxation techniques, and seeking mental health support when needed.

Stress Management for Healthcare Professionals:

Healthcare professionals play a critical role in caring for others, but their demanding work can take a toll on their mental health. We will discuss strategies for managing stress in the healthcare field, such as building resilience, practicing self-care, and seeking support from colleagues and professionals.

Stress Management for Veterans and Military Personnel:

Veterans and military personnel often face unique stressors due to their service experiences. We will explore the connection between stress and mental health in this context and provide coping strategies specifically tailored to this audience. From seeking peer support to utilizing specialized mental health services, we aim to empower veterans and military personnel to effectively manage stress and protect their mental well-being.

Stress Management for Seniors and Retirees:

Even in retirement, stress can still be a significant factor in one's life. We will discuss the potential stressors faced by seniors and retirees and provide strategies for managing stress during this life stage. From engaging in hobbies to maintaining social connections, we will explore practical ways to promote mental health and well-being.

Stress Management for Individuals with Chronic Illnesses or Disabilities:

Living with a chronic illness or disability can be incredibly challenging, and stress often accompanies these conditions. We will address the unique stressors faced by individuals in this situation and offer practical strategies for managing stress, including self-care practices, seeking support groups, and utilizing adaptive coping techniques.

Stress Management for Couples and Relationships:

Stress can take a toll on relationships, leading to conflicts and decreased intimacy. We will explore the impact of stress on couples and provide techniques for managing stress together. From effective communication to prioritizing quality time, we will delve into strategies for nurturing relationships under pressure.

In this subchapter, we have covered the multifaceted connection between stress and mental health in various contexts. By understanding the relationship between these two factors, individuals from all walks of life can take proactive steps towards managing stress and protecting their mental well-being. Remember, stress is inevitable, but with the right tools and strategies, it is possible to thrive even in the face of life's pressures.

The Importance of Stress Management in Relationships

In today's fast-paced and demanding world, stress has become an inevitable part of our daily lives. From work pressures to family responsibilities, we are constantly bombarded with stressors that can take a toll on our mental and physical well-being. This is particularly true for couples and relationships, where stress can often put a strain on even the strongest bonds.

Understanding and managing stress in relationships is crucial for maintaining a healthy and fulfilling partnership. Stress can lead to a range of negative effects, including increased tension, decreased communication, and a diminished ability to resolve conflicts. Without effective stress management techniques, couples may find themselves feeling overwhelmed and disconnected from one another.

Workplace stress management is a key aspect of maintaining a healthy relationship. Many individuals spend a significant portion of their day at work, and job-related stress can spill over into their personal lives. By learning how to manage workplace stress and finding ways to support each other in coping with it, couples can prevent it from negatively impacting their relationship.

Parents and caregivers face unique stressors that can strain their relationship. Juggling childcare responsibilities, financial pressures, and personal needs can be overwhelming. Stress management techniques tailored to the specific challenges faced by parents and caregivers can help them navigate these difficulties and maintain a strong bond with their partner.

For students and academics, stress can arise from the demands of coursework, exams, and research. Learning effective stress management techniques can not only enhance academic performance but also prevent stress from affecting personal relationships.

Entrepreneurs and business owners often face high levels of stress due to the demands of running a business. Incorporating stress management strategies into their lives can help them strike a balance between work and personal life, reducing the strain on their relationships.

Stress management is equally important for athletes, sports professionals, healthcare professionals, veterans, seniors, individuals with chronic illnesses or disabilities, and all other individuals who experience stress in their daily lives. By prioritizing stress management and seeking support when needed, individuals can strengthen their relationships and prevent stress from becoming a barrier to their happiness and well-being.

In "Love Under Pressure: Stress Management for Couples and Relationships in the Modern World," readers will discover practical strategies and tools to effectively manage stress in their relationships. From communication techniques to mindfulness exercises, this book provides a comprehensive guide to navigating the challenges of stress and creating a resilient and loving partnership.

By understanding the importance of stress management in relationships and implementing proven techniques, couples can build a foundation of trust, support, and understanding. With these tools in hand, they can weather any storm and enjoy a fulfilling, harmonious, and stress-free relationship.

Chapter 2: Workplace Stress Management

Identifying Sources of Stress in the Workplace

In today's fast-paced and demanding work environment, stress has become an inevitable part of our lives. Whether you are an employee, an entrepreneur, or a business owner, understanding and managing workplace stress is crucial for maintaining a healthy work-life balance. In this subchapter, we will explore the different sources of stress that can affect individuals in various professional settings.

One common source of workplace stress is excessive workload. The pressure to meet deadlines, handle multiple tasks, and achieve high performance can be overwhelming. Additionally, conflicts with colleagues or superiors, lack of control over one's work, and long working hours can also contribute to stress levels.

For parents and caregivers, balancing work responsibilities with family obligations can be extremely challenging. Juggling between attending to the needs of children or elderly parents while meeting work demands can lead to chronic stress. Understanding how to manage these responsibilities effectively is essential for maintaining one's mental and emotional well-being.

Students and academics often face the stress of exams, assignments, and deadlines. The pressure to perform well academically, coupled with the fear of failure, can lead to anxiety and overwhelm. Developing effective study habits, time management skills, and seeking support from peers and professionals can significantly reduce stress levels in this niche.

Entrepreneurs and business owners face unique stressors such as financial uncertainty, managing employees, and making crucial business decisions. The responsibility of running a business can be incredibly demanding, leading to high levels of stress. Learning effective stress management techniques and seeking support from mentors and business networks can help alleviate the pressures faced by entrepreneurs.

Athletes and sports professionals face tremendous pressure to perform at their best. The physical demands, competition, and expectations from coaches, fans, and sponsors can contribute to high levels of stress. Implementing stress management techniques such as mindfulness, visualization, and seeking support from sports psychologists can help athletes maintain their mental and emotional well-being.

Healthcare professionals, veterans, seniors, and individuals with chronic illnesses or disabilities also face unique stressors in their respective fields. Understanding the specific challenges faced by these individuals and offering tailored stress management strategies can greatly improve their quality of life.

Lastly, couples and relationships can also be affected by workplace stress. Balancing career aspirations, communication breakdowns, and lack of quality time together can strain relationships. Learning effective communication techniques, setting boundaries, and prioritizing self-care as a couple can help in managing stress and maintaining a healthy relationship.

In conclusion, identifying the sources of stress in the workplace is the first step towards effective stress management. By understanding the unique stressors faced by individuals in different professional settings, we can offer targeted strategies to help individuals and couples navigate the challenges and pressures of the modern work environment.

Strategies for Managing Work-Related Stress

Work-related stress is a common issue that affects individuals across various industries and professions. The demands of modern-day work can often lead to overwhelming feelings of stress and anxiety. However, it is essential to recognize that there are effective strategies to manage and reduce work-related stress. This subchapter aims to provide practical tips and techniques to help individuals in different walks of life cope with the pressures of work and maintain a healthy work-life balance.

Understanding and Managing Stress:

To effectively manage work-related stress, it is crucial to understand its causes and effects. This section will explore the different sources of stress in the workplace and provide insights into identifying personal triggers. By recognizing the signs and symptoms of stress, individuals can take proactive steps towards managing it and preventing it from escalating.

Workplace Stress Management:

This section is specifically designed to address the unique challenges faced by individuals in a professional setting. It will delve into effective time management techniques, setting realistic goals, and establishing healthy boundaries between work and personal life. Additionally, it will provide guidance on effective communication and conflict resolution strategies to minimize workplace stress.

Stress Management for Parents and Caregivers:

Juggling the responsibilities of work and family can be particularly stressful for parents and caregivers. This section will offer practical advice on prioritizing tasks, delegating responsibilities, and creating a support system. It will also provide insights into effective parenting techniques that can reduce stress and promote a harmonious work-life balance.

Stress Management for Students and Academics:

Students and academics often face immense pressure to perform academically, resulting in high levels of stress. This section will provide guidance on effective study techniques, time management skills, and coping mechanisms to handle the demands of education. It will also explore strategies for maintaining a healthy work-life balance and managing stress during exam periods.

Stress Management for Entrepreneurs and Business Owners:

Running a business or being an entrepreneur comes with its unique set of stressors. This section will focus on strategies for setting realistic expectations, prioritizing tasks, and managing the pressures of entrepreneurship. It will also provide insights into effective leadership and delegation skills to reduce stress and maintain a successful business.

Stress Management for Athletes and Sports Professionals:

Athletes and sports professionals often face immense pressure to perform at their best. This section will address the unique challenges they face and provide strategies for managing stress in high-pressure situations. It will explore techniques such as visualization, mindfulness, and self-care practices that can enhance performance and reduce stress.

Stress Management for Healthcare Professionals:

Healthcare professionals are exposed to high levels of stress due to the nature of their work. This section will provide strategies for managing emotional exhaustion, setting boundaries, and practicing self-care. It will also offer guidance on effective communication and teamwork in a healthcare setting.

Stress Management for Veterans and Military Personnel:

This section will address the specific stressors faced by veterans and military personnel and provide strategies for managing post-traumatic stress disorder (PTSD) and the challenges of transitioning into civilian life. It will explore resources available to support mental health and well-being and provide tips for maintaining a healthy work-life balance.

Stress Management for Seniors and Retirees:

Even in retirement, individuals can experience stress related to financial concerns, health issues, and adjusting to a new routine. This section will offer guidance on stress management techniques specifically tailored for seniors and retirees. It will explore the importance of staying socially engaged, pursuing hobbies, and seeking support from loved ones.

Stress Management for Individuals with Chronic Illnesses or Disabilities:

Individuals with chronic illnesses or disabilities often face additional stressors related to their health conditions. This section will provide strategies for managing stress while dealing with ongoing medical challenges. It will focus on self-care practices, effective communication with healthcare providers, and seeking support from support groups or counseling services.

Stress Management for Couples and Relationships:

Work-related stress can significantly impact relationships. This section will provide strategies for couples to navigate stress together and maintain a healthy relationship. It will explore effective communication techniques, setting shared goals, and supporting each other during stressful times.

In conclusion, this subchapter aims to provide a comprehensive guide to managing work-related stress. By implementing these strategies, individuals from various backgrounds can reduce stress levels, enhance well-being, and improve their overall quality of life.

Creating a Healthy Work-Life Balance

In today's fast-paced and demanding world, achieving a healthy work-life balance is more important than ever. Many of us find ourselves constantly juggling multiple responsibilities, leading to stress, burnout, and strained relationships. However, with some practical strategies and mindset shifts, it is possible to create a harmonious balance between work and personal life.

Understanding and Managing Stress:

Stress is an inevitable part of life, but it is crucial to recognize its impact on our physical and mental well-being. This subchapter will explore the different types of stress and provide effective techniques for managing and reducing stress levels. By understanding the root causes of stress and implementing stress management techniques, individuals can regain control over their lives and create a healthier work-life balance.

Workplace Stress Management:

The modern workplace can be a breeding ground for stress and anxiety. This section will delve into the common workplace stressors and offer practical tips for managing stress in the professional environment. From time management strategies to setting boundaries, readers will learn how to navigate the pressures of work while still preserving their personal lives.

Stress Management for Parents and Caregivers:

Parents and caregivers often find themselves overwhelmed by the demands of their roles. This subchapter will provide guidance on how to balance parenting responsibilities with personal needs. It will explore effective time management techniques, self-care practices, and strategies for maintaining open communication within the family unit.

Stress Management for Students and Academics:

Students and academics face unique stressors such as exams, deadlines, and research pressures. This section will address the specific challenges faced by this group and offer practical advice on managing stress effectively. From time management skills to study techniques, readers will gain insights into how to prioritize their well-being while excelling academically.

Stress Management for Entrepreneurs and Business Owners:

Entrepreneurs and business owners often find themselves consumed by their work, leading to neglect of personal relationships and self-care. This subchapter will provide strategies for achieving a healthy work-life balance in the entrepreneurial world. From delegating tasks to setting realistic goals, readers will learn how to create a thriving business while still maintaining a fulfilling personal life.

Stress Management for Couples and Relationships:

Lastly, this subchapter will explore how stress impacts relationships and offer practical advice for couples. From effective communication to shared responsibilities, readers will learn how to support each other in managing stress and fostering a healthy, loving relationship.

In "Creating a Healthy Work-Life Balance," readers from various walks of life will find practical strategies and insights to help them navigate the challenges of stress and achieve a more fulfilling and harmonious life. Whether you are a student, a parent, a business owner, or anyone seeking a better work-life balance, this subchapter is your guide to finding peace and happiness amidst the pressures of the modern world.

Effective Communication in the Workplace

In today's fast-paced and competitive world, effective communication in the workplace is crucial for success and overall well-being. Whether you are an employee, manager, or business owner, understanding and implementing effective communication strategies can help reduce stress, enhance relationships, and foster a positive work environment.

Communication is not just about exchanging information; it is about understanding and being understood. It involves both verbal and non-verbal cues, active listening, and empathy. By mastering these skills, you can enhance your communication and reduce misunderstandings, conflicts, and stress in the workplace.

One important aspect of effective communication is active listening. This means giving your full attention to the person speaking and avoiding distractions. It involves not only hearing the words but also understanding the underlying emotions and intentions. By being an active listener, you demonstrate respect and build trust with your colleagues, superiors, and subordinates.

Another vital aspect of effective communication is empathy. This means putting yourself in others' shoes and understanding their perspectives and feelings. By practicing empathy, you can create a supportive and inclusive work environment where everyone feels valued and understood.

Furthermore, clear and concise communication is essential to avoid misunderstandings and confusion. Be mindful of your language, tone, and body language when communicating in the workplace. Use simple and straightforward language, ask for clarification when needed, and be aware of non-verbal cues such as facial expressions and gestures.

In addition, effective communication requires open and honest feedback. Providing constructive feedback and actively seeking feedback from others can help improve performance and foster personal and professional growth. Remember to be respectful and specific when giving feedback, focusing on behaviors rather than personal attacks.

Lastly, technology has revolutionized the way we communicate in the workplace. While it offers convenience and efficiency, it can also lead to misinterpretations and miscommunication. Be mindful of the medium you choose for your communication and consider the best method for conveying your message accurately.

In conclusion, effective communication in the workplace is essential for reducing stress, enhancing relationships, and fostering a positive work environment. By practicing active listening, empathy, clear and concise communication, open feedback, and mindful use of technology, you can improve your communication skills and create a harmonious and productive workplace. Remember, effective communication is a skill that can be learned and mastered, benefiting not only your professional life but also your personal relationships.

Building Resilience and Coping Mechanisms

In today's fast-paced and demanding world, stress has become an inevitable part of our lives. Whether you are a student struggling with academic pressures, a healthcare professional dealing with life-or-death situations, or a business owner trying to navigate the challenges of entrepreneurship, stress can take a toll on your well-being and relationships. However, by developing resilience and adopting effective coping mechanisms, you can not only manage stress but also thrive in the face of adversity.

Resilience, put simply, is the ability to bounce back from setbacks and adapt to change. It is an essential quality that can be cultivated and strengthened over time. In this subchapter, we will explore various strategies and techniques to build resilience in different areas of life, ensuring that you are equipped to face any challenge that comes your way.

For individuals grappling with workplace stress, we will delve into effective stress management techniques tailored to the demands of the corporate world. From time management and prioritization to setting realistic goals and establishing healthy boundaries, you will discover practical tools to navigate work-related stress and maintain a healthy work-life balance.

Parents and caregivers often find themselves overwhelmed by the demands of their roles. We will explore coping mechanisms specifically designed to help parents and caregivers manage stress and maintain their own well-being while caring for others. From seeking support networks to self-care practices, you will learn how to prioritize your mental and emotional health in the midst of parental responsibilities.

Students and academics face unique stressors, such as exams, deadlines, and the pressure to excel academically. This subchapter will provide strategies to manage academic stress effectively, including time management, study techniques, and stress-reducing practices that promote overall well-being.

Entrepreneurs and business owners face numerous challenges that can lead to burnout and chronic stress. We will address the specific stressors they encounter and provide coping mechanisms to help them navigate the entrepreneurial journey with resilience and grace.

We will also delve into stress management techniques tailored for athletes and sports professionals, healthcare professionals, veterans and military personnel, seniors and retirees, individuals with chronic illnesses or disabilities, and couples and relationships. Each section will offer practical tips and strategies to build resilience and cope with stress in these unique contexts.

By implementing the tools and techniques discussed in this subchapter, you will not only enhance your ability to manage stress but also empower yourself to thrive in the face of adversity. Remember, resilience is not about eliminating stress but rather about building the capacity to adapt, grow, and maintain well-being in the midst of life's challenges.

Chapter 3: Stress Management for Parents and Caregivers

Balancing Parenting Responsibilities and Stress

Parenting is undoubtedly one of the most rewarding experiences in life, but it also comes with its fair share of stress and challenges. In today's fast-paced world, where both parents often have full-time jobs and numerous other responsibilities, finding a balance between parenting and managing stress can feel like an uphill battle. However, it is essential for the well-being of both parents and children.

In this subchapter, we will explore effective strategies to help parents navigate the complexities of parenting while managing stress. Whether you are a working parent, a caregiver, or an entrepreneur, these techniques will provide valuable insights into finding equilibrium in your life.

First and foremost, it is crucial to recognize the signs of stress and acknowledge its impact on your overall well-being. Understanding the source of your stress and its effects will enable you to develop targeted coping mechanisms. We will delve into various stress management techniques, such as mindfulness, meditation, and exercise, which have proven to be highly effective in reducing stress levels.

We will also address the unique stressors faced by parents and caregivers, such as the pressure to excel at work while being present for their children. This section will provide practical tips on setting boundaries, delegating tasks, and fostering open communication with your partner. Additionally, we will discuss the importance of self-care and how taking care of your own needs is not selfish but a necessary component of effective parenting.

For students and academics, we will explore methods to balance the demands of education with the responsibilities of parenthood. From time management strategies to seeking support from professors and peers, we will equip you with the tools needed to thrive academically while nurturing your family.

Entrepreneurs and business owners often face unique stressors, as they juggle the demands of their businesses and their families. In this section, we will discuss strategies to delegate tasks, set realistic goals, and create a supportive network to ensure both personal and professional success.

We will also address the specific stressors faced by athletes, healthcare professionals, veterans, seniors, individuals with chronic illnesses or disabilities, and couples. Each group will benefit from tailored advice and coping mechanisms to help them navigate the unique challenges they face.

By finding a healthy balance between parenting responsibilities and managing stress, you can create a harmonious environment for both yourself and your family. This subchapter aims to provide practical guidance and support for individuals from all walks of life, empowering them to lead fulfilling lives while effectively managing stress.

Coping with the Demands of Caregiving

Caregiving is a noble and selfless act of love and compassion. Whether you are caring for a child, an aging parent, a spouse, or someone with a chronic illness or disability, the demands of caregiving can be overwhelming and stressful. In this subchapter, we will explore effective strategies to help you cope with the challenges that come with being a caregiver.

Understanding and Managing Stress:

Caregiving often involves a tremendous amount of physical, emotional, and mental stress. It is crucial to recognize the signs of stress and take steps to manage it effectively. This subchapter will provide you with practical techniques such as deep breathing exercises, mindfulness practices, and stress-reducing activities to help you find balance and resilience amidst the demands of caregiving.

Workplace Stress Management:

Many caregivers juggle their caregiving responsibilities with their professional lives. This can lead to added stress and pressure. We will discuss strategies for setting boundaries, communicating with your employer, and seeking support from colleagues. Additionally, we will provide tips for time management and prioritization, allowing you to maintain a healthy work-life balance while fulfilling your caregiving duties.

Stress Management for Parents and Caregivers:

Being a parent is a full-time job in itself, and when combined with caregiving responsibilities, it can quickly become overwhelming. This subchapter will address the unique challenges that parents face when caring for a child with special needs or a chronic illness. We will discuss strategies for self-care, building a support network, and seeking professional help when needed.

Stress Management for Students and Academics:

Balancing the demands of caregiving with academic pursuits can be incredibly challenging. This subchapter will provide strategies to help students and academics manage their stress levels effectively. From time management techniques to setting realistic goals, we will explore ways to navigate the unique pressures faced by students and academics who are also caregivers.

Stress Management for Entrepreneurs and Business Owners:

Running a business or being an entrepreneur requires immense dedication and focus. When combined with caregiving responsibilities, it can feel like an impossible feat. In this section, we will offer practical advice for entrepreneurs and business owners on managing their stress levels, delegating tasks, and finding support systems to maintain a healthy work-life integration.

Stress Management for Healthcare Professionals:

Healthcare professionals are often at the forefront of caregiving, facing immense pressure and emotional challenges. This subchapter will address the specific stressors faced by healthcare professionals and offer techniques to manage stress effectively. From setting boundaries to practicing self-care, healthcare professionals will find practical strategies to enhance their well-being.

Stress Management for Veterans and Military Personnel:

For veterans and military personnel, transitioning from a high-stress environment to caregiving can be overwhelming. This subchapter will explore strategies to help veterans and military personnel manage the demands of caregiving while addressing the unique challenges they face. From seeking support to accessing resources, we will provide guidance tailored to their specific needs.

Stress Management for Seniors and Retirees:

Many seniors and retirees find themselves in the role of caregiver for their spouses or aging family members. This subchapter will offer practical tips for managing the stress of caregiving while prioritizing self-care. We will explore ways for seniors and retirees to maintain their own well-being while providing care for their loved ones.

Stress Management for Individuals with Chronic Illnesses or Disabilities:

Individuals with chronic illnesses or disabilities often experience significant stress while managing their own health and caregiving responsibilities. This subchapter will provide support and coping strategies for individuals in this situation. We will discuss self-care techniques, accessing support networks, and finding a balance between personal needs and caregiving duties.

Stress Management for Couples and Relationships:

Caregiving can place a strain on relationships, and it is crucial to prioritize the health of your partnership while navigating the demands of caregiving. In this section, we will offer guidance for couples on communication, setting boundaries, and finding quality time together. We will explore strategies to strengthen your relationship and navigate the challenges of caregiving as a team.

In conclusion, the demands of caregiving can be overwhelming, but with the right strategies and support, you can effectively manage stress and maintain your well-being. This subchapter provides practical advice and techniques tailored to various audiences, ensuring that caregivers from all walks of life can find solace and strength as they navigate the challenges of caregiving.

Utilizing Support Systems and Resources

In our modern world, stress has become a common and often overwhelming aspect of our daily lives. From the workplace to personal relationships, stress can take a toll on our overall well-being. However, it is essential to remember that you are not alone in this journey. By utilizing support systems and resources available to you, you can effectively manage and overcome stress.

Understanding and Managing Stress

To begin, it is crucial to understand the nature of stress and its impact on our lives. This subchapter explores the various causes and symptoms of stress, helping readers identify stress triggers in their own lives. By acknowledging and understanding stress, you can take the first step towards managing it effectively.

Workplace Stress Management

For individuals facing stress in the workplace, this section provides valuable insights and strategies. From creating a healthy work-life balance to developing effective communication skills, readers will discover practical tools to navigate the challenges of their professional lives. Additionally, we explore techniques for managing work-related stress, such as time management, delegation, and setting boundaries.

Stress Management for Parents and Caregivers

Parents and caregivers often face unique stressors, balancing the demands of their personal and family lives. This chapter offers guidance on effective parenting techniques, communication with children, and self-care practices. Discover how to prioritize your mental and emotional well-being while ensuring a nurturing environment for your loved ones.

Stress Management for Students and Academics

Students and academics are no strangers to stress, with the pressures of exams, assignments, and deadlines. This section provides valuable tips on time management, study techniques, and self-care practices. Learn how to maintain a healthy work-life balance and achieve academic success without compromising your mental health.

Stress Management for Entrepreneurs and Business Owners

Entrepreneurs and business owners face unique stressors in their pursuit of success. This subchapter offers practical advice on managing stress while running a business. From effective organization and delegation to maintaining healthy relationships with colleagues and clients, readers will gain valuable insights into balancing their professional and personal lives.

Stress Management for Athletes and Sports Professionals

Athletes and sports professionals often face immense pressure to perform at their best. This section explores techniques to manage stress in the sports arena, from mental preparation and visualization to effective goal-setting and team communication. Discover how to maintain peak performance while prioritizing your mental and emotional well-being.

Stress Management for Healthcare Professionals

Healthcare professionals play a crucial role in society, often facing high levels of stress and burnout. This subchapter provides strategies for managing stress in healthcare settings, including self-care practices, boundary-setting, and seeking support. Learn how to prioritize your well-being while providing compassionate care to others.

Stress Management for Veterans and Military Personnel

Veterans and military personnel may face unique stressors due to their service. This section offers resources and techniques to manage stress related to combat experiences, transition to civilian life, and post-traumatic stress disorder (PTSD). Discover coping mechanisms, therapy options, and support networks specifically tailored to veterans and military personnel.

Stress Management for Seniors and Retirees

As we age, stress can take on new forms and challenges. This chapter explores stress management techniques for seniors and retirees, including maintaining social connections, engaging in meaningful activities, and prioritizing self-care. Learn how to navigate the unique stressors of this life stage and embrace a fulfilling and stress-free retirement.

Stress Management for Individuals with Chronic Illnesses or Disabilities

Individuals living with chronic illnesses or disabilities often face additional stressors. This section provides strategies for managing stress related to health challenges, including self-care practices, support networks, and adaptive coping mechanisms. Discover how to maintain a positive mindset and quality of life while navigating the complexities of chronic illness or disability.

Stress Management for Couples and Relationships

Finally, this chapter explores stress management techniques for couples and relationships. From effective communication and conflict resolution to maintaining intimacy and connection, readers will discover strategies to strengthen their relationships while navigating life's stressors. Learn how to support each other through challenging times and foster a loving and resilient partnership.

In conclusion, by utilizing the support systems and resources available, individuals in various niches can effectively manage and overcome stress. This subchapter addresses the unique challenges faced by different groups, providing valuable insights and practical strategies. Remember, you are not alone in this journey, and with the right tools, you can thrive in the face of stress.

Self-Care for Parents and Caregivers

Parenting and caregiving can be incredibly rewarding, but it also comes with its fair share of stress and challenges. As a parent or caregiver, it's important to prioritize your own well-being and practice self-care to ensure you can effectively support and care for others. In this subchapter, we will explore various strategies and techniques that can help parents and caregivers manage stress and maintain their own mental and physical health.

One of the most important aspects of self-care is recognizing and acknowledging your own needs. Many parents and caregivers tend to put their own needs last, but it's crucial to remember that you can't pour from an empty cup. Take time for yourself and engage in activities that bring you joy and relaxation, whether it's reading a book, taking a walk, or pursuing a hobby. Prioritize self-care as an essential part of your daily routine.

Another key aspect of self-care is seeking support and building a network of people who can provide assistance. Don't be afraid to ask for help when you need it, whether it's from family members, friends, or support groups. Surround yourself with individuals who understand the challenges you face and can offer guidance or simply lend a listening ear.

Managing stress is also vital for parents and caregivers. Find healthy coping mechanisms to deal with stress, such as exercise, meditation, or deep breathing exercises. Practice mindfulness and be present in the moment, focusing on what you can control rather than worrying about the unknown. Set realistic expectations for yourself and learn to delegate tasks to alleviate some of the pressure.

Additionally, maintaining a healthy work-life balance is crucial. Set boundaries between work and personal life, and make time for activities that bring you joy and rejuvenation. Remember that taking care of yourself is not selfish; it's essential for your own well-being and for being able to provide adequate care for your loved ones.

In this subchapter, we have explored various strategies and techniques to help parents and caregivers practice self-care and manage stress. By prioritizing your own well-being and implementing these strategies, you can ensure that you are better equipped to handle the demands of parenting and caregiving. Remember, taking care of yourself is not a luxury, but a necessity for maintaining healthy relationships and overall well-being.

Nurturing Relationships amidst Stressful Roles

In today's fast-paced and demanding world, stress has become an integral part of our daily lives. Whether you are a parent juggling multiple responsibilities, an athlete striving for peak performance, or a healthcare professional constantly under pressure, stress can take a toll on your relationships. However, it is essential to understand that stress doesn't have to define your relationships; instead, you can nurture them even amidst the most challenging roles.

This chapter of "Love Under Pressure: Stress Management for Couples and Relationships in the Modern World" is dedicated to helping you understand and manage stress within the context of your relationships. Whether you are a student, an entrepreneur, a caregiver, or someone with a chronic illness, the principles shared here will apply to your unique circumstances.

The first step in nurturing relationships amidst stressful roles is acknowledging the impact of stress on your interactions. Stress can lead to increased irritability, reduced patience, and decreased communication, which can strain even the strongest of bonds. By recognizing these stress-induced patterns, you can consciously work towards breaking them.

Next, it is crucial to prioritize self-care. Stress management begins with taking care of yourself physically, emotionally, and mentally. Engage in activities that help you relax and recharge, such as exercise, meditation, or spending time in nature. When you prioritize your well-being, you can bring a healthier and more positive energy to your relationships.

Communication is the cornerstone of any successful relationship, particularly when stress is involved. Establish open and honest lines of communication with your partner, family members, or friends. Express your needs, concerns, and feelings, and encourage them to do the same. By fostering a safe space for dialogue, you can strengthen your relationships and find support during challenging times.

Additionally, finding coping mechanisms together can be extremely beneficial. Explore stress management techniques that work for both of you. This could include engaging in shared activities, seeking professional help, or finding new hobbies that provide a sense of relaxation and connection. By facing stress as a team, you can build resilience and deepen your bond.

Lastly, it is essential to celebrate small victories and express gratitude regularly. In the midst of stress, it's easy to overlook the positive aspects of your relationships. By acknowledging and appreciating each other's efforts, you can cultivate a culture of gratitude and reinforce the love and support you share.

Remember, stress is inevitable, but its impact on your relationships can be managed. By understanding and managing stress within the context of your roles, you can nurture your relationships and create a stronger foundation for love and support. Embrace the tools and strategies shared in this chapter, and embark on a journey towards healthier and more fulfilling relationships amidst the pressures of the modern world.

Chapter 4: Stress Management for Students and Academics

Academic Pressure and Stress in Educational Settings

In today's fast-paced and competitive world, academic pressure has become a significant source of stress for individuals across various age groups. From students and parents to educators and professionals, the demands of the educational system can take a toll on one's mental and emotional well-being. This chapter aims to shed light on the academic pressure and stress experienced in educational settings and provide practical strategies for managing and reducing this stress.

For students and academics, the pressure to excel academically can be overwhelming. The constant need to meet high expectations, perform well in exams, and maintain a competitive edge can lead to stress, anxiety, and even burnout. This section will explore the causes and consequences of academic pressure, as well as effective stress management techniques specifically tailored for students and academics.

Parents and caregivers also face unique challenges when it comes to managing the academic stress of their children. Balancing their own expectations with the well-being of their children can be a delicate task. This subchapter will provide guidance on how parents can support their children without adding unnecessary pressure and stress, fostering a healthy and balanced approach to education.

Furthermore, entrepreneurs, business owners, athletes, healthcare professionals, veterans, seniors, individuals with chronic illnesses or disabilities, and even couples in relationships can all experience academic pressure and stress in different ways. This chapter will explore the specific stressors faced by these niches and offer targeted strategies to manage and alleviate their stress.

Understanding the underlying causes of academic pressure and stress is paramount to effectively managing it. By addressing the root causes and implementing stress management techniques, individuals can create a healthier and more balanced approach to education. This chapter will equip readers with practical tools and knowledge to navigate the educational landscape without compromising their mental and emotional well-being.

Whether you are a student, parent, educator, professional, or caregiver, this chapter aims to provide valuable insights and strategies to help you understand and manage the academic pressure and stress that can often accompany educational pursuits. By implementing these techniques, individuals can forge a path towards success without sacrificing their mental health and overall well-being.

Effective Time Management and Study Techniques

In today's fast-paced world, stress has become a common companion for many individuals and relationships. Whether you are a student, parent, caregiver, athlete, or professional, the demands of daily life can often leave you feeling overwhelmed and stretched thin. This subchapter aims to provide valuable insights and practical strategies for effective time management and study techniques, which are essential tools in managing and reducing stress.

When it comes to time management, understanding your priorities is crucial. Start by identifying your goals and breaking them down into smaller, manageable tasks. This will allow you to allocate your time effectively and ensure that you are focusing on what truly matters. Additionally, learning to say "no" and setting boundaries is essential. It is important to recognize that you can't do everything and that it is okay to delegate or decline certain tasks to maintain a healthy work-life balance.

For students and academics, effective study techniques can significantly impact overall performance and reduce stress. One technique to consider is the Pomodoro Technique, where you work for a set period (typically 25 minutes) and then take a short break. This method helps maintain focus and prevents burnout. Additionally, creating a dedicated study space, setting specific goals, and utilizing active learning techniques such as flashcards or group discussions can enhance comprehension and retention.

Entrepreneurs and business owners often face unique challenges when it comes to time management. Prioritizing tasks, delegating responsibilities, and utilizing technology tools can help streamline operations and reduce stress. Time-blocking, a technique where you allocate specific time slots for different tasks, can also be highly effective in maximizing productivity.

For individuals in healthcare, veterans, seniors, or those with chronic illnesses or disabilities, time management can be even more critical. It is essential to plan and schedule appointments and treatments effectively, while also allowing time for self-care and relaxation. Utilizing assistive technologies and seeking support from caregivers or loved ones can also help alleviate the burden.

Lastly, for couples and relationships, effective time management is vital for maintaining a healthy connection. Scheduling quality time together, setting boundaries between work and personal life, and actively listening and supporting each other's needs can help foster a stronger bond and reduce stress within the relationship.

In conclusion, effective time management and study techniques are essential skills for managing stress in various aspects of life. By understanding priorities, setting boundaries, and utilizing strategies specific to your niche, you can create a more balanced and fulfilling life while minimizing the negative effects of stress.

Coping with Exam Stress and Performance Anxiety

Exams are a common source of stress and anxiety for many individuals, regardless of their age or profession. Whether you are a student, an entrepreneur, a healthcare professional, or someone with a chronic illness, the pressure to perform well can be overwhelming. In this subchapter, we will explore effective strategies to cope with exam stress and performance anxiety.

Understanding and Managing Stress:

Stress is a natural response to challenging situations, and exams can be particularly stressful. It is crucial to understand the impact of stress on our bodies and minds. We will delve into the various physical and psychological symptoms of stress and provide practical techniques to manage and reduce stress levels.

Workplace Stress Management:

For professionals who have to juggle multiple responsibilities, exams can add an extra layer of stress. We will discuss strategies to manage workplace stress while preparing for exams. From time management techniques to creating a supportive work environment, we will provide practical tips to minimize stress and maximize productivity.

Stress Management for Parents and Caregivers:

Parents and caregivers often experience their own stress and anxiety while supporting their children or loved ones during exams. We will explore effective strategies to cope with these unique challenges, including maintaining open communication, setting realistic expectations, and practicing self-care.

Stress Management for Students and Academics:

Students and academics face tremendous pressure to excel in their studies and research. This subchapter will provide valuable insights into managing exam stress, including effective study techniques, time management strategies, and mental preparation exercises.

Stress Management for Athletes and Sports Professionals:

Athletes and sports professionals not only deal with physical demands but also face the pressure of performing at their best during competitions. We will explore specific techniques to manage exam stress while maintaining peak performance, including visualization, positive self-talk, and relaxation techniques.

Stress Management for Healthcare Professionals, Veterans, and Military Personnel:

The healthcare field, as well as veterans and military personnel, often face high-stress environments. This subchapter will address the unique challenges they face during exams and provide tailored strategies to manage stress effectively.

Stress Management for Seniors, Retirees, and Individuals with Chronic Illnesses or Disabilities:

Seniors, retirees, and individuals with chronic illnesses or disabilities may encounter additional stress during exams. We will discuss strategies to cope with these challenges, including seeking support, adapting study methods, and practicing self-compassion.

Stress Management for Couples and Relationships:

Exams can place strain on relationships, particularly when both partners are facing exam stress. We will explore ways to support each other during this time, maintain open communication, and prioritize self-care and quality time together.

By implementing the strategies discussed in this subchapter, you can effectively cope with exam stress and performance anxiety, regardless of your personal or professional circumstances. Remember, managing stress is a lifelong skill that can benefit all aspects of your life.

Seeking Support from Peers and Mentors

In times of stress and pressure, it is crucial to have a support system that understands and empathizes with your struggles. This support can come from both peers and mentors, who can provide guidance, encouragement, and a safe space to express your concerns. In this subchapter, we will explore the importance of seeking support from peers and mentors and how it can benefit individuals in various aspects of their lives.

Understanding and Managing Stress: Stress is a common experience that affects individuals from all walks of life. By connecting with peers who are going through similar challenges, you can gain a sense of belonging and validation. Sharing your stressors and listening to others' experiences can offer new perspectives and coping strategies, helping you navigate stress more effectively.

Workplace Stress Management: In the fast-paced and demanding world of work, seeking support from peers and mentors can be invaluable. Peers can offer a listening ear, while mentors can provide guidance on career development and stress management techniques specific to your industry. Together, they can help you navigate workplace challenges, maintain a healthy work-life balance, and prevent burnout.

Stress Management for Parents and Caregivers: Parenting and caregiving can be overwhelming, particularly when combined with other responsibilities. Peers who are also parents or caregivers can provide emotional support, practical advice, and a sense of camaraderie. Mentors who have successfully raised children or managed caregiving responsibilities can offer valuable insights, helping you navigate the unique stressors of this role.

Stress Management for Students and Academics: The academic journey can be highly stressful, with constant deadlines, exams, and high expectations. Peers can offer study tips, share resources, and serve as accountability partners. Mentors, such as professors or professionals in your field, can provide guidance on career paths, research opportunities, and stress management techniques tailored to the academic environment.

Stress Management for Entrepreneurs and Business Owners: Running a business or being an entrepreneur can be both exciting and stressful. Connecting with peers who have similar experiences can provide a network of support, collaboration opportunities, and a space to share challenges and successes. Mentors who have built successful businesses can offer guidance, strategic advice, and help navigate the unique stressors of entrepreneurship.

Stress Management for Athletes and Sports Professionals: Competitive sports can take a toll on an individual's physical and mental well-being. Peers who understand the demands of training and competition can provide support, motivation, and a listening ear. Mentors, such as seasoned athletes or sports psychologists, can offer guidance on performance enhancement, stress reduction techniques, and managing the pressures of high-level sports.

Stress Management for Healthcare Professionals: Those working in healthcare face unique stressors, including long hours, emotional strain, and high stakes. Connecting with peers and mentors in the healthcare field can provide a support system that understands the challenges and provides a safe space to debrief and seek guidance. Mentors who have navigated successful careers in healthcare can offer insights into work-life balance, self-care, and managing stress in a demanding environment.

Stress Management for Veterans and Military Personnel: Military life can be extremely challenging, with frequent deployments, traumatic experiences, and the pressure to perform under stressful conditions. Peers who have served or are currently serving can provide a sense of camaraderie and understanding. Mentors who have transitioned successfully into civilian life can offer guidance on stress management, career transitions, and accessing support services.

Stress Management for Seniors and Retirees: Aging comes with its own set of stressors, including health concerns, financial worries, and social isolation. Connecting with peers who are in a similar stage of life can provide support, companionship, and the opportunity to share experiences and wisdom. Mentors who have successfully navigated retirement can offer guidance on finding purpose, staying active, and managing stress in this new phase of life.

Stress Management for Individuals with Chronic Illnesses or Disabilities: Living with a chronic illness or disability can be physically and emotionally challenging. Peers who share similar experiences can provide a support system that understands the unique stressors and offers empathy and encouragement. Mentors who have successfully managed their conditions can offer insights into coping strategies, self-care, and finding a fulfilling life despite the challenges.

Stress Management for Couples and Relationships: Relationships can be a source of both joy and stress. Seeking support from peers who are in committed relationships can offer a sense of validation and advice on navigating common challenges. Mentors who have successfully maintained healthy relationships can provide guidance on effective communication, conflict resolution, and stress management techniques tailored to couples.

In conclusion, seeking support from peers and mentors is crucial for managing stress in various aspects of life. Whether you are dealing with workplace stress, parenting challenges, academic pressures, or any other stressor, connecting with individuals who understand and empathize with your experiences can provide invaluable support, guidance, and a sense of belonging. By reaching out to your peers and seeking mentors who have successfully navigated similar challenges, you can build a support system that empowers you to thrive in the face of stress.

Maintaining Well-Being while Pursuing Education

In today's fast-paced and demanding world, pursuing education can often add to the stress and pressure we already experience in our daily lives. Whether you are a student, an academic, a parent, an entrepreneur, a healthcare professional, a veteran, or someone with a chronic illness, it is essential to prioritize your well-being while undertaking educational pursuits. This subchapter aims to provide practical strategies and insights to help you navigate the challenges and maintain well-being throughout your educational journey.

First and foremost, it is crucial to recognize and understand the signs of stress. Stress can manifest in various ways, including physical, emotional, and behavioral symptoms. By being aware of these signs, you can take proactive steps to manage stress before it overwhelms you. Additionally, understanding the causes of stress specific to your situation, whether it be academic pressure or work-related demands, can help you develop targeted coping mechanisms.

One effective strategy for managing stress is to establish a routine that incorporates self-care activities. This can include exercise, mindfulness practices, adequate sleep, and healthy eating habits. Engaging in activities that bring you joy and relaxation, such as hobbies or spending quality time with loved ones, can also help alleviate stress and improve overall well-being.

Furthermore, seeking support from your social network can make a significant difference in managing stress. Surrounding yourself with understanding and empathetic individuals, such as friends, family, or support groups, can provide emotional support and practical advice. Additionally, consider seeking professional help, such as therapy or counseling, if you find yourself overwhelmed or struggling to cope with stress.

Another vital aspect of maintaining well-being while pursuing education is setting realistic goals and managing expectations. It is essential to prioritize and manage your time effectively, ensuring that you have a healthy work-life balance. Learning to say no to additional commitments that may overwhelm you is also crucial.

Lastly, maintaining open and honest communication with your partner, if applicable, can significantly impact your well-being and relationship. Discussing your educational pursuits, setting boundaries, and finding ways to support each other can help alleviate stress within the relationship and strengthen your bond.

In conclusion, pursuing education can be a challenging endeavor, but it is possible to maintain well-being throughout the process. By recognizing the signs of stress, establishing self-care routines, seeking support, managing expectations, and nurturing relationships, you can successfully manage stress and thrive in your educational journey. Remember, taking care of yourself is essential, and your well-being should always be a priority.

Chapter 5: Stress Management for Entrepreneurs and Business Owners

The Unique Stressors Faced by Entrepreneurs

Entrepreneurs are a unique breed of individuals who take on the challenges of starting and running their own businesses. While the rewards of entrepreneurship can be immense, the journey is often fraught with various stressors that are distinct to this career path. In this subchapter, we will explore the unique stressors faced by entrepreneurs and provide strategies for managing and navigating these challenges.

One of the primary stressors faced by entrepreneurs is the constant pressure to succeed. Unlike employees who can rely on a steady paycheck, entrepreneurs have their financial well-being tied directly to the success of their ventures. This can lead to a constant fear of failure and the need to constantly prove oneself. The stress of financial uncertainty and the weight of responsibility can take a toll on an entrepreneur's mental and emotional well-being.

Another stressor specific to entrepreneurs is the need to wear multiple hats. In the early stages of a business, entrepreneurs often find themselves taking on various roles, from marketing and sales to operations and customer service. The sheer volume of responsibilities can be overwhelming and lead to feelings of burnout and exhaustion.

Furthermore, entrepreneurs often face a lack of work-life balance. The demands of running a business can consume every waking moment, leaving little time for personal relationships, self-care, and leisure activities. This imbalance can put a strain on relationships and lead to feelings of isolation and loneliness.

Additionally, entrepreneurs often face a unique set of external pressures. They must navigate the competitive business landscape, stay up-to-date with industry trends, and constantly innovate to stay ahead. This constant pressure to stay relevant and adapt to changes can lead to high levels of stress and anxiety.

To effectively manage these unique stressors, entrepreneurs must prioritize self-care and stress management techniques. This can include setting boundaries, delegating tasks, and seeking support from mentors or fellow entrepreneurs who understand the journey. Developing a strong support network and practicing stress-reducing activities such as exercise, meditation, and hobbies can also help in managing the demands of entrepreneurship.

In conclusion, entrepreneurs face a unique set of stressors that can impact their mental, emotional, and physical well-being. By understanding these stressors and implementing effective stress management strategies, entrepreneurs can navigate the challenges of entrepreneurship while maintaining their health and well-being.

Strategies for Managing Business-Related Stress

In today's fast-paced and competitive world, stress has become an inevitable part of our lives, especially when it comes to managing business-related pressures. Whether you are an entrepreneur, a business owner, a professional, or an employee, finding effective strategies to cope with stress is crucial for your overall well-being and success. In this subchapter, we will explore a range of strategies tailored to help individuals in various niches manage business-related stress.

Understanding and Managing Stress: The first step towards managing stress is understanding it. We will delve into the science of stress, its impact on our minds and bodies, and how to identify the warning signs. By gaining a deeper understanding of stress, individuals can develop personalized stress management strategies that work for them.

Workplace Stress Management: This section will focus on techniques specifically designed for individuals facing stress in the workplace. We will explore strategies like time management, setting realistic goals, effective communication, and creating work-life balance. Additionally, we will discuss mindfulness and relaxation techniques to help individuals cope with the demands of their jobs.

Stress Management for Parents and Caregivers: Juggling the responsibilities of work and family can be overwhelming. This section will provide practical tips on managing stress for parents and caregivers. We will discuss the importance of self-care, setting boundaries, seeking support, and finding time for relaxation and rejuvenation.

Stress Management for Students and Academics: Students and academics often face immense pressure to excel academically. We will explore strategies to help them manage their stress effectively, such as time management, study techniques, stress-reducing exercises, and seeking support from peers and mentors.

Stress Management for Entrepreneurs and Business Owners: Running a business or being an entrepreneur comes with its unique set of challenges. This section will provide insights into managing the stress associated with entrepreneurship, including strategies for dealing with uncertainty, overcoming burnout, and maintaining a healthy work-life balance.

Stress Management for Athletes and Sports Professionals: Athletes and sports professionals face intense physical and mental stress. We will discuss techniques to manage performance anxiety, stress associated with competition, injury recovery, and maintaining mental well-being.

Stress Management for Healthcare Professionals: Healthcare professionals often experience high levels of stress due to the demanding nature of their jobs. This section will address strategies for managing stress in the healthcare field, including self-care practices, setting boundaries, and seeking support from colleagues and mentors.

Stress Management for Veterans and Military Personnel: Veterans and military personnel face unique stressors. We will explore strategies tailored to their specific needs, including coping with traumatic experiences, transitioning to civilian life, and seeking mental health support.

Stress Management for Seniors and Retirees: Even in retirement, stress can still be present. This section will cover strategies for seniors and retirees to manage stress, including staying socially engaged, pursuing hobbies, maintaining physical health, and seeking emotional support.

Stress Management for Individuals with Chronic Illnesses or Disabilities: Individuals with chronic illnesses or disabilities often face additional stressors. We will discuss strategies to manage stress in these circumstances, such as self-compassion, stress-reducing exercises, support groups, and seeking professional help.

Stress Management for Couples and Relationships: Stress can take a toll on relationships. This section will focus on strategies for couples to navigate stress together, including effective communication, shared responsibilities, quality time, and supporting each other's well-being.

By implementing these strategies, individuals in various niches can effectively manage their business-related stress, leading to improved well-being, better relationships, and increased success in their respective fields. Remember, managing stress is a lifelong journey, and it is essential to find what works best for you.

Achieving Work-Life Integration as an Entrepreneur

As an entrepreneur, finding a balance between work and personal life can often seem like an impossible task. The demands of running a business, coupled with the pressures of everyday life, can leave you feeling overwhelmed and stressed. However, with the right strategies and mindset, it is possible to achieve work-life integration and find harmony in both areas of your life.

One of the first steps towards achieving work-life integration is setting clear boundaries. As an entrepreneur, it's easy to let work seep into every aspect of your life. However, it's important to establish designated work hours and stick to them. This means avoiding checking emails or taking business calls outside of these hours, allowing yourself time to focus on your personal life and recharge.

Another important aspect of work-life integration is learning to delegate and ask for help. As entrepreneurs, we often feel like we need to do everything ourselves to ensure it gets done right. However, this mentality only leads to burnout and increased stress levels. Learning to trust and delegate tasks to others not only frees up your time but also allows you to focus on the things that truly matter.

Finding time for self-care is also crucial in achieving work-life integration. As entrepreneurs, we tend to prioritize our businesses over our own well-being. However, neglecting self-care only leads to decreased productivity and increased stress levels. It's important to schedule regular breaks, engage in activities that bring you joy, and prioritize your physical and mental health.

Additionally, creating a support system can greatly contribute to work-life integration. Surrounding yourself with like-minded individuals who understand the challenges of entrepreneurship can provide invaluable support and guidance. Whether it's joining networking groups, attending conferences, or seeking out a mentor, having a support system can help alleviate stress and provide a sense of belonging.

Lastly, learning to let go of perfectionism is essential in achieving work-life integration. As entrepreneurs, we often strive for perfection in everything we do, which can lead to unnecessary stress and burnout. Understanding that it's okay to make mistakes and that perfection is an unattainable goal allows us to focus on progress rather than perfection.

In conclusion, achieving work-life integration as an entrepreneur is possible with the right strategies and mindset. Setting clear boundaries, delegating tasks, prioritizing self-care, creating a support system, and letting go of perfectionism are all essential steps towards finding harmony between work and personal life. By implementing these strategies, entrepreneurs can reduce stress levels, increase productivity, and ultimately lead a more fulfilling and balanced life.

Building a Supportive Network and Seeking Assistance

In times of stress, it is crucial to have a strong support system in place. The people we surround ourselves with can greatly impact our ability to manage stress and navigate through challenging situations. This subchapter explores the importance of building a supportive network and seeking assistance when needed, offering valuable insights for individuals and couples facing stress in various aspects of their lives.

Understanding and Managing Stress: Stress is a universal experience, and understanding it is the first step towards effective stress management. This section explores the different sources of stress and provides guidance on how to identify and address them. It emphasizes the importance of seeking support from family, friends, or professionals who can offer guidance and understanding.

Workplace Stress Management: The modern workplace is often a breeding ground for stress, but it doesn't have to be. This section provides strategies for managing workplace stress, including building strong relationships with colleagues, seeking assistance from mentors or supervisors, and utilizing available resources such as employee assistance programs. It emphasizes the importance of open communication and seeking help when needed.

Stress Management for Parents and Caregivers: Parents and caregivers face unique stressors that can impact their well-being. This section offers guidance on building a support network, including friends, family members, and support groups. It emphasizes the importance of self-care and seeking assistance from professionals when necessary, reminding parents and caregivers that they don't have to face stress alone.

Stress Management for Students and Academics: Students and academics often experience high levels of stress due to academic pressures. This section explores the importance of seeking assistance from teachers, counselors, or support services on campus. It provides tips for building a support network among peers and emphasizes the importance of self-care and time management for reducing stress.

Stress Management for Entrepreneurs and Business Owners: Running a business can be incredibly stressful, and entrepreneurs and business owners often face unique challenges. This section offers guidance on building a supportive network of fellow entrepreneurs, mentors, or business coaches. It emphasizes the importance of delegating tasks, seeking assistance when needed, and prioritizing self-care to manage stress effectively.

Stress Management for Couples and Relationships: Stress can put a strain on relationships, but having a supportive partner can make all the difference. This section explores strategies for building a strong support system within a relationship, including open communication, active listening, and seeking couples therapy when necessary. It emphasizes the importance of supporting each other through stressful times.

No matter the niche or specific stressors one may face, building a supportive network and seeking assistance are essential for effective stress management. This subchapter provides valuable insights, strategies, and resources for individuals and couples to navigate through stress and build a strong support system. Remember, you don't have to face stress alone – reach out and lean on your support network when needed.

Sustaining Mental and Emotional Well-Being in Business

In the fast-paced and demanding world of business, it is crucial to prioritize mental and emotional well-being. The pressures and stressors that come with running a business can take a toll on individuals, affecting not only their personal lives but also their professional success. This subchapter aims to provide practical tips and strategies for sustaining mental and emotional well-being in the business world, benefiting a wide range of audiences, including entrepreneurs, professionals, parents, caregivers, students, athletes, healthcare professionals, veterans, seniors, individuals with chronic illnesses or disabilities, and couples in relationships.

Understanding and Managing Stress is the first step towards maintaining mental and emotional well-being. It is essential to recognize the signs of stress and adopt effective stress management techniques. This chapter will explore different stress management strategies tailored to the unique needs of various niches, such as workplace stress management, stress management for parents and caregivers, stress management for students and academics, stress management for athletes and sports professionals, stress management for healthcare professionals, stress management for veterans and military personnel, stress management for seniors and retirees, stress management for individuals with chronic illnesses or disabilities, and stress management for couples and relationships.

The subchapter will delve into specific techniques and tools for managing stress, including mindfulness practices, meditation, breathing exercises, physical activity, and time management strategies. Additionally, it will address the importance of maintaining a healthy work-life balance, setting boundaries, and seeking support when needed. The content will highlight the detrimental effects of chronic stress on mental and emotional well-being, emphasizing the significance of self-care and stress reduction techniques.

Furthermore, the subchapter will shed light on the impact of stress on relationships and offer guidance on how couples can support each other in times of stress. It will explore effective communication strategies, conflict resolution techniques, and ways to foster resilience and emotional connection within relationships.

By implementing the strategies and techniques presented in this subchapter, individuals from various backgrounds can cultivate and sustain their mental and emotional well-being in the challenging world of business. Whether it is managing workplace stress, balancing responsibilities as a parent or caregiver, coping with the demands of academia, or navigating the unique challenges faced by athletes, veterans, healthcare professionals, seniors, individuals with chronic illnesses or disabilities, and couples, this content aims to provide practical and valuable insights for all.

Chapter 6: Stress Management for Athletes and Sports Professionals

The Pressure of Performance in Sports

Sports have always been a source of excitement, passion, and camaraderie. Whether you are a professional athlete or a weekend warrior, the pressure to perform can be overwhelming. In this subchapter, we will explore the unique challenges athletes face and provide strategies to manage the pressure of performance.

For athletes, the pressure to excel is constant. Whether it's the expectation to win championships, set personal records, or secure lucrative contracts, the stakes are high. This pressure can manifest in various ways, such as anxiety, self-doubt, and fear of failure. Understanding and managing stress in sports is crucial for optimal performance and overall well-being.

One key aspect of managing performance pressure is recognizing the importance of mental and emotional well-being. Athletes must prioritize self-care and stress management techniques to maintain a healthy mindset. Techniques such as mindfulness, visualization, and deep breathing can help athletes stay calm and focused, even in high-pressure situations.

Furthermore, it is essential for athletes to set realistic goals and maintain a healthy perspective. While striving for excellence is admirable, it is equally important to embrace the journey and appreciate the process. By setting achievable goals, athletes can reduce unnecessary stress and foster a positive mindset.

Workplace stress management techniques can also be applied to the world of sports. Athletes can benefit from techniques such as time management, prioritization, and effective communication. By developing these skills, athletes can better balance their training, competition, and personal lives, reducing stress and enhancing overall performance.

Additionally, the pressure of performance in sports can have a significant impact on personal relationships. Athletes must maintain open lines of communication with their partners, family, and friends to ensure a healthy support system. Seeking professional help, such as couples counseling or therapy, can also be beneficial in navigating the unique challenges of balancing a relationship and a demanding sports career.

In conclusion, the pressure of performance in sports is a significant challenge that athletes face. By understanding and managing stress, setting realistic goals, prioritizing mental and emotional well-being, and maintaining healthy relationships, athletes can thrive both on and off the field. Remember, sports should be a source of joy and fulfillment, and by managing the pressure of performance, athletes can truly love what they do under pressure.

Techniques for Managing Pre-Competition Stress

Pre-competition stress is a common experience faced by individuals across various domains, including sports, work, academics, and relationships. In order to perform at our best, it is important to effectively manage this stress and channel it into positive energy. This subchapter explores various techniques to help individuals cope with pre-competition stress and achieve optimal performance.

One effective technique is deep breathing and relaxation exercises. Deep breathing helps calm the mind and relax the body, reducing anxiety and tension. By focusing on slow, deep breaths, individuals can regulate their heart rate and promote a sense of calmness.

Incorporating relaxation techniques such as progressive muscle relaxation or guided imagery can further enhance relaxation and mental preparedness.

Another technique is mental rehearsal or visualization. By mentally rehearsing the upcoming competition, individuals can reduce anxiety and enhance their performance. Visualizing successful outcomes and imagining themselves performing at their best can boost confidence and reinforce positive beliefs. Practicing visualization regularly can help individuals feel more prepared and confident when facing the actual competition.

Positive self-talk is another powerful technique for managing pre-competition stress. Our thoughts greatly influence our emotions and behaviors, so it is important to cultivate a positive mindset. Encouraging and supportive self-talk can help individuals build resilience, maintain focus, and boost confidence. Affirmations and positive statements can be repeated before and during the competition to counteract negative thoughts and promote a positive mindset.

Physical activity and exercise are also effective stress management techniques. Engaging in regular physical activity helps release endorphins, our body's natural mood boosters, and reduces stress hormones. Incorporating exercise into daily routines can help individuals manage pre-competition stress, improve overall well-being, and increase resilience.

Lastly, social support plays a crucial role in managing pre-competition stress. Talking to trusted friends, family members, or coaches who understand the pressures of competition can provide a sense of comfort and reassurance. Sharing concerns and seeking advice or encouragement from others can help individuals gain perspective and alleviate stress.

In conclusion, managing pre-competition stress is essential for individuals across various domains. By incorporating techniques such as deep breathing, mental rehearsal, positive self-talk, physical activity, and social support, individuals can effectively cope with pre-competition stress and optimize their performance. These techniques can be applied by athletes, students, professionals, caregivers, individuals with chronic illnesses, couples, and anyone seeking to manage and overcome stress in their lives.

Recovering from Injuries and Handling Setbacks

In the journey of life, setbacks and injuries are inevitable. Whether it's a physical injury, a setback in your career, or a strain in your relationships, these challenges can leave us feeling overwhelmed and uncertain about the future. However, it is essential to remember that setbacks are a natural part of growth, and with the right mindset and strategies, you can bounce back stronger than ever.

Recovering from injuries, both physical and emotional, requires patience, resilience, and a holistic approach. In this subchapter, we will explore the various techniques and tools to help you navigate through these difficult times.

For individuals dealing with physical injuries, we will delve into the importance of seeking professional help, following a structured rehabilitation plan, and adopting a positive mindset. We will also address the emotional aspect of recovery, providing guidance on managing frustration, maintaining self-care, and seeking support from loved ones.

In the workplace, setbacks can lead to increased stress and decreased productivity. We will discuss effective stress management techniques, including time management, setting boundaries, and seeking support from colleagues and supervisors. We will also explore strategies to regain confidence and motivation after setbacks, such as setting realistic goals and focusing on personal growth.

For parents and caregivers, setbacks can be particularly challenging as they juggle multiple responsibilities. We will provide practical tips on managing stress, finding balance, and seeking support from other parents or professional networks.

Students and academics often face setbacks in their educational journey. We will explore effective stress management techniques for managing academic pressure, dealing with setbacks in exams or projects, and maintaining a healthy work-life balance.

Entrepreneurs and business owners face unique challenges and setbacks in their ventures. We will discuss strategies for managing stress, adapting to change, and staying resilient in the face of setbacks.

Athletes, sports professionals, and healthcare professionals often experience setbacks due to injuries or high-pressure situations. We will delve into techniques for physical and mental recovery, including rehabilitation, goal-setting, and seeking support from coaches or therapists.

For veterans, military personnel, seniors, individuals with chronic illnesses or disabilities, and couples in relationships, setbacks can be even more challenging. We will provide guidance on seeking professional help, building a support network, and nurturing resilience in the face of adversity.

Remember, setbacks are not permanent roadblocks. With the right mindset, support, and strategies, you can overcome any setback and emerge stronger than before. Together, let's navigate the path to recovery and build a life filled with love and resilience under pressure.

Balancing Athletic Career and Personal Life

In today's fast-paced world, finding a balance between a successful athletic career and personal life can be challenging. Athletes face unique stressors, such as intense training schedules, competition pressure, and the constant need to perform at their best. This subchapter aims to provide valuable insights and practical strategies for athletes, as well as anyone looking to maintain a healthy balance between their professional and personal lives.

Understanding and Managing Stress: Stress is an inevitable part of life, and athletes are no exception. This section explores the different sources of stress in an athletic career and provides tips on how to recognize and manage stress effectively. It emphasizes the importance of self-care and stress-reducing techniques to maintain overall well-being.

Workplace Stress Management: Athletes often consider their training environment as their workplace. This section delves into the unique stressors faced by athletes in their training and competition settings. It offers strategies to create a supportive and positive training environment, promoting teamwork and open communication.

Stress Management for Parents and Caregivers: Athletes who are also parents or caregivers face the added challenge of balancing their athletic career with their responsibilities at home. This section provides guidance on how to find support systems and delegate tasks effectively, ensuring that both their personal and professional lives receive the attention they deserve.

Stress Management for Students and Academics: Many athletes are also students or academics, juggling their athletic career with their educational pursuits. This section offers practical advice on time management, setting priorities, and maintaining a healthy work-life balance while pursuing academic excellence.

Stress Management for Entrepreneurs and Business Owners: Athletes who have ventures outside of their athletic careers face unique stressors associated with managing their businesses. This section explores strategies to delegate tasks, set boundaries, and maintain a healthy work-life integration, ensuring success in both their professional and personal endeavors.

Stress Management for Healthcare Professionals: Athletes often rely on a team of healthcare professionals to optimize their performance and recovery. This section discusses the importance of open communication and collaboration between athletes and their healthcare providers, ensuring a holistic approach to stress management and overall well-being.

Stress Management for Veterans and Military Personnel: This section acknowledges the unique challenges faced by veterans and military personnel transitioning into athletic careers. It provides guidance on how to navigate the demands of both their athletic pursuits and their military background, promoting resilience and self-care.

Stress Management for Seniors and Retirees: As athletes age or transition into retirement, they may face new stressors and challenges. This section offers strategies to adapt to these changes, focusing on maintaining physical and mental well-being, finding new passions, and embracing a balanced and fulfilling lifestyle.

Stress Management for Individuals with Chronic Illnesses or Disabilities: Athletes with chronic illnesses or disabilities face additional obstacles in finding balance. This section provides insights into adaptive training techniques, self-care strategies, and building a support network, empowering athletes to thrive despite their unique circumstances.

Stress Management for Couples and Relationships: Balancing an athletic career and personal life often impacts relationships. This section explores effective communication, setting boundaries, and finding quality time for partners to maintain a healthy and fulfilling relationship.

In "Love Under Pressure: Stress Management for Couples and Relationships in the Modern World," this subchapter offers practical guidance and strategies for athletes and individuals from various niches to achieve a healthy balance between their athletic careers and personal lives. By understanding and managing stress effectively, athletes can enhance their overall well-being, performance, and relationships, creating a harmonious and fulfilling life both on and off the field.

Mental Training for Peak Performance

In today's fast-paced and demanding world, stress has become an inevitable part of our lives. Whether you are a student, a business owner, an athlete, a healthcare professional, or a caregiver, the pressures and demands can often leave you feeling overwhelmed and burnt out. However, there is a way to manage and even thrive under pressure – through mental training for peak performance.

This subchapter of "Love Under Pressure: Stress Management for Couples and Relationships in the Modern World" explores the power of mental training and how it can be applied to various aspects of life. Whether you are looking to enhance your personal performance, improve your relationships, or find ways to manage stress effectively, mental training can be a game-changer.

Understanding and managing stress is the first step towards achieving peak performance. By recognizing the triggers and symptoms of stress, individuals can learn to develop resilience and coping strategies. This subchapter provides practical techniques and exercises for understanding and managing stress in different contexts, such as the workplace, parenting, academics, entrepreneurship, sports, healthcare, the military, and retirement. The content is tailored to the specific needs of each niche, offering insights and strategies that can be easily implemented.

Furthermore, mental training for peak performance highlights the importance of building mental strength and agility. It explores the power of mindfulness, visualization, goal-setting, and self-talk in enhancing performance and reducing stress. By training the mind to stay focused, positive, and resilient, individuals can unlock their full potential and achieve peak performance in their respective domains.

This subchapter also emphasizes the significance of support systems and relationships in stress management. It discusses how couples can train together, support each other, and build resilience as a team. The content delves into effective communication, conflict resolution, and emotional support techniques that enhance the well-being of both individuals and their relationships.

Overall, this subchapter on mental training for peak performance offers a comprehensive guide to managing stress and achieving excellence in various areas of life. Whether you are a stressed-out student, an overwhelmed caregiver, a burnt-out professional, or a couple seeking to strengthen your relationship, this content provides practical tools and insights to help you thrive under pressure. So, embark on the journey of mental training and unlock your potential for peak performance and a fulfilling life.

Chapter 7: Stress Management for Healthcare Professionals

Stressors in the Healthcare Industry

The healthcare industry is undoubtedly one of the most demanding and high-pressure sectors in the modern world. From doctors and nurses to administrators and support staff, everyone involved faces a myriad of stressors that can take a toll on their mental and physical well-being. In this subchapter, we will explore the unique stressors faced by healthcare professionals and provide valuable insights on managing stress in this challenging field.

One of the primary stressors in the healthcare industry is the heavy workload. Healthcare professionals often work long hours, sometimes even overnight, juggling multiple patients and complex cases. The constant pressure to provide the best care while dealing with time constraints can lead to burnout and chronic stress. It is crucial for healthcare professionals to prioritize self-care and find healthy ways to cope with the demands of their job.

Another significant stressor in the healthcare industry is the emotional toll of dealing with patients' suffering and loss. Healthcare professionals witness human suffering on a daily basis, which can be emotionally draining and lead to compassion fatigue. It is essential for healthcare professionals to establish strong support networks and seek therapy or counseling when needed to process their emotions effectively.

Additionally, the healthcare industry is no stranger to organizational and administrative stressors. Constant changes in healthcare policies, insurance regulations, and the need to keep up with advancements in medical technology can create additional pressure for healthcare professionals. Developing effective time management and organizational skills can help alleviate some of these stressors.

Moreover, healthcare professionals face the challenge of maintaining a work-life balance. The demanding nature of their job often leaves little time for personal life, leading to strained relationships and increased stress levels. It is crucial for healthcare professionals to set boundaries, prioritize self-care, and seek support from their loved ones to maintain a healthy work-life balance.

This subchapter aims to provide healthcare professionals with practical strategies to manage stress effectively. By understanding the unique stressors in the healthcare industry and implementing stress management techniques, healthcare professionals can improve their overall well-being and provide better care to their patients.

Whether you are a healthcare professional, a caregiver, or simply interested in understanding and managing stress in the healthcare industry, this subchapter will provide valuable insights and practical tips to help you navigate the challenging world of healthcare while maintaining your mental and physical health.

Strategies for Coping with Emotional Toll

In today's fast-paced modern world, stress has become an inevitable part of our lives. Whether you are a busy professional, a parent, a student, an athlete, or someone dealing with a chronic illness, stress can take a toll on your emotional well-being. To maintain a healthy and fulfilling life, it is crucial to develop effective strategies to cope with the emotional burden that stress brings. In this chapter, we will explore various techniques that can help you manage your emotions and find balance amidst life's challenges.

One of the key strategies for coping with emotional toll is self-care. Taking care of yourself physically, mentally, and emotionally is essential for managing stress. Engage in activities that bring you joy and relaxation, such as exercise, meditation, hobbies, or spending quality time with loved ones. Prioritizing self-care will help you recharge and build resilience against stressors.

Another important approach is seeking support from others. Building a strong support system can provide comfort and guidance during difficult times. Reach out to your friends, family, or colleagues and share your feelings and concerns. In some cases, professional help from therapists or counselors may be necessary to navigate through complex emotions. Remember, seeking support is a sign of strength, not weakness.

Emotional intelligence plays a vital role in managing stress. By becoming aware of your emotions and understanding their impact on your well-being, you can develop better coping mechanisms. Practice mindfulness and self-reflection to identify triggers and patterns in your emotional responses. Once you have this awareness, you can choose healthier ways to express and manage your emotions effectively.

Additionally, adopting stress management techniques such as time management, setting boundaries, and practicing relaxation techniques can greatly alleviate the emotional toll. Learn to prioritize your tasks, delegate responsibilities, and say no when necessary. Incorporate relaxation techniques like deep breathing exercises, progressive muscle relaxation, or guided imagery into your daily routine to calm your mind and reduce stress.

Lastly, maintaining open and honest communication in your relationships is crucial for managing emotional stress together. Share your feelings with your partner, family, or friends, and encourage them to express themselves as well. By fostering a supportive and understanding environment, you can navigate through stress as a team.

Remember, coping with emotional toll is an ongoing process. It requires self-awareness, practice, and patience. By implementing these strategies into your life, you can cultivate emotional resilience and find harmony amidst the challenges of the modern world.

Maintaining Boundaries and Preventing Burnout

In today's fast-paced and demanding world, stress has become an unwelcome companion in our lives. From managing work responsibilities to taking care of our families and maintaining our relationships, it is easy to feel overwhelmed and burnt out. But it doesn't have to be this way. In this subchapter, we will explore the importance of maintaining boundaries and share practical strategies to prevent burnout.

Understanding and Managing Stress

Stress is a natural response to challenging situations, but when left unmanaged, it can take a toll on our mental and physical well-being. By understanding the triggers and signs of stress, you can take proactive steps to manage it effectively. We will discuss various stress management techniques such as deep breathing, meditation, exercise, and seeking support from loved ones or professionals.

Workplace Stress Management

Work-related stress is a common issue that affects many individuals. Whether you're an employee or a business owner, it is crucial to establish healthy boundaries to prevent burnout. We will provide tips on time management, setting realistic goals, delegating tasks, and creating a work-life balance that promotes overall well-being.

Stress Management for Parents and Caregivers

Parents and caregivers often face unique stressors, juggling multiple responsibilities and putting others' needs before their own. This subchapter will offer guidance on self-care, effective communication, setting boundaries with children, and seeking support from other parents or support groups.

Stress Management for Students and Academics

Academic life can be highly demanding, leading to stress and burnout among students and academics. We will explore techniques such as time management, prioritization, effective study habits, and seeking mentorship or counseling to help students and academics navigate the pressures of their educational journey.

Stress Management for Entrepreneurs and Business Owners

Running a business or being an entrepreneur comes with its own set of challenges and stressors. This section will focus on strategies to manage stress, improve work-life integration, delegate tasks, seek feedback and support, and build a resilient mindset to thrive in the fast-paced business world.

Stress Management for Couples and Relationships

Relationships are not immune to stress, and neglecting one's well-being can strain even the strongest bonds. We will delve into effective communication, setting boundaries, prioritizing quality time together, and seeking couples therapy or relationship coaching to foster a healthy and resilient partnership.

From healthcare professionals and athletes to veterans and individuals with chronic illnesses, this subchapter will provide tailored strategies for specific niches. By implementing these techniques and maintaining healthy boundaries, you can prevent burnout, enhance your well-being, and cultivate fulfilling relationships in the modern world.

Remember, stress is a part of life, but managing it is within your control. Together, let's embark on a journey towards love, resilience, and stress-free living.

Self-Care for Healthcare Providers

In the fast-paced and demanding world of healthcare, it is easy for healthcare providers to put their own needs on the backburner as they prioritize the well-being of their patients. However, neglecting self-care can lead to burnout, decreased job satisfaction, and even compromised patient care. That is why it is crucial for healthcare providers to prioritize their own self-care in order to better serve others.

Understanding and managing stress is of utmost importance for healthcare providers. The constant exposure to high-pressure situations, long working hours, and emotional strain can take a toll on their well-being. It is essential for healthcare providers to recognize the signs of stress and implement effective stress management techniques. This can include activities such as exercise, meditation, engaging in hobbies, and seeking support from friends and family.

Workplace stress management is another key aspect of self-care for healthcare providers. Creating a positive work environment, fostering open communication, and implementing strategies to manage workload and prevent burnout are essential. Healthcare organizations should prioritize the well-being of their staff by offering training programs on stress management, providing access to mental health resources, and promoting work-life balance.

Parents and caregivers who are healthcare providers face unique challenges. Juggling the demands of work and family can be overwhelming. It is essential for these individuals to establish boundaries, delegate tasks, and seek support from their partner, family members, or professional caregivers. Taking time for themselves, whether it is engaging in self-care activities or seeking therapy, is crucial for maintaining their own well-being.

Similarly, healthcare providers who are students and academics face the pressure of balancing their studies, research, and clinical work. They should prioritize self-care by managing their time effectively, seeking support from mentors or advisors, and practicing stress management techniques such as mindfulness and self-reflection.

Entrepreneurs and business owners in the healthcare industry often face unique stressors. They must not only manage their own well-being but also the well-being of their employees and the success of their business. Prioritizing self-care through time management, delegating tasks, and seeking support from professionals in the field can help alleviate stress and maintain a healthy work-life balance.

Athletes and sports professionals who are also healthcare providers face the challenge of physical and mental exhaustion. Engaging in self-care activities such as regular exercise, proper nutrition, and restorative practices like yoga or meditation can help them manage stress and maintain peak performance.

Healthcare professionals who are veterans or military personnel may face additional stressors related to their service. It is crucial for these individuals to seek support from fellow veterans, mental health professionals, and support groups. Engaging in self-care activities that promote relaxation and well-being can also be beneficial.

Seniors, retirees, and individuals with chronic illnesses or disabilities who are healthcare providers must prioritize their own self-care to manage their conditions effectively. This can include seeking support from healthcare professionals, engaging in activities that bring joy and relaxation, and practicing self-compassion.

Lastly, stress management for couples and relationships is important for healthcare providers who are in committed partnerships. Open communication, shared responsibilities, and quality time together can help strengthen their relationship and provide support during stressful times.

In conclusion, self-care for healthcare providers is crucial for their own well-being as well as the quality of care they provide to their patients. Prioritizing stress management, workplace well-being, and personal self-care activities can help healthcare providers thrive in their demanding roles and lead fulfilling lives both inside and outside the workplace.

Promoting Healthy Relationships with Patients

In the fast-paced and stressful world we live in, it can be easy to overlook the importance of healthy relationships, especially when it comes to healthcare professionals and their patients. However, fostering a positive connection with patients is not only essential for their well-being but also for the overall success of their treatment. In this subchapter, we will explore the significance of promoting healthy relationships with patients and provide practical tips on how to achieve this goal.

For healthcare professionals, understanding and managing stress is crucial. By prioritizing their own stress management, they can create a positive environment for their patients. When healthcare professionals are calm and composed, patients feel more comfortable and are more likely to open up about their concerns. This openness allows for better communication and a deeper understanding of the patient's needs.

Workplace stress management is another important aspect to consider. Healthcare professionals often face high-pressure situations, tight schedules, and challenging work environments. By implementing stress management techniques such as mindfulness, self-care, and setting boundaries, they can maintain their well-being and provide better care to their patients.

Parents and caregivers also play a significant role in promoting healthy relationships with patients, especially when it comes to children or individuals with chronic illnesses or disabilities. By being supportive, empathetic, and involved in their loved one's healthcare journey, parents and caregivers can create a sense of safety and trust, which greatly contributes to the patient's overall well-being.

Students and academics, entrepreneurs and business owners, athletes and sports professionals, veterans and military personnel, seniors and retirees – everyone can benefit from understanding and managing stress in their relationships with patients. By practicing active listening, showing empathy, and demonstrating respect, individuals in these niches can establish a strong foundation for a healthy patient-provider relationship.

Lastly, this subchapter also addresses the importance of stress management for couples and relationships. Couples who support each other's healthcare journeys, communicate effectively, and prioritize self-care are more likely to navigate the challenges of illness or disability together successfully.

In conclusion, promoting healthy relationships with patients is vital for healthcare professionals, patients, and their loved ones. By understanding and managing stress, whether it be workplace stress, stress in relationships, or stress related to specific niches, individuals can create an environment that fosters trust, open communication, and ultimately, better patient outcomes.

Chapter 8: Stress Management for Veterans and Military Personnel

Understanding the Unique Stressors of Military Life

Military life is a unique experience that comes with its own set of challenges and stressors. Whether you are a military service member yourself or have a loved one serving in the military, it is important to understand and recognize the unique stressors that come with this lifestyle. In this subchapter, we will explore the various stressors faced by military personnel and their families, and provide strategies for managing and coping with these challenges.

One of the primary stressors of military life is the constant uncertainty and unpredictability. Deployments, frequent relocations, and separation from loved ones can create immense stress and anxiety. Military families often live with the constant fear and worry about the safety and well-being of their loved ones. This subchapter will provide insights and tips for managing the emotional toll of these uncertainties, including effective communication strategies and building a strong support network.

The demanding nature of military work can also take a toll on service members' mental and physical health. The pressures of combat, long hours, and the need to constantly be on high alert can lead to chronic stress, anxiety, and even post-traumatic stress disorder (PTSD). We will discuss techniques for managing stress in high-pressure situations, accessing mental health resources, and promoting overall well-being for military personnel.

For military families, the frequent moves and transitions can disrupt routines and social connections. Adjusting to new environments, schools, and communities can be challenging and isolating. This subchapter will provide practical advice on managing the stress of relocation, maintaining a sense of stability and routine, and building a support system in new locations.

Additionally, military life often requires juggling multiple roles and responsibilities. Service members may struggle with the dual demands of their military duties and their family responsibilities. This subchapter will explore strategies for effective time management, setting boundaries, and finding a healthy balance between work and personal life.

Finally, we will address the unique challenges faced by military couples and relationships. Frequent separations, communication barriers, and the strain of military life can put a significant strain on relationships. This subchapter will provide guidance on fostering open and effective communication, managing conflict, and strengthening the bonds in military relationships.

Understanding and managing the unique stressors of military life is essential for the well-being of military personnel and their families. By providing practical strategies and insights, this subchapter aims to support individuals and couples in navigating the challenges of military life and maintaining healthy and thriving relationships.

Transitioning to Civilian Life and Managing Stress

Introduction:

Transitioning from a military career to civilian life can be a challenging and stressful process. This subchapter aims to provide guidance and strategies to help individuals effectively manage the stress associated with this transition. Whether you are a veteran, a military personnel, or a family member supporting a loved one, this chapter will offer valuable insights into understanding and managing stress during this phase of life.

Understanding the Transition:

The transition from military to civilian life involves significant changes in routines, identities, and responsibilities. It is important to recognize that this period can trigger a range of emotions, including anxiety, confusion, and even loss. By understanding the common challenges associated with this transition, individuals can better equip themselves to manage stress and adapt to their new life.

Coping Strategies for Managing Stress:

1. Seek Support: Connect with fellow veterans, support groups, or organizations that specialize in assisting individuals transitioning to civilian life. Sharing experiences and seeking guidance from those who have gone through a similar journey can provide immense comfort and support.

2. Build a Routine: Establishing a new routine can help create a sense of stability and purpose. Set realistic goals, prioritize tasks, and gradually integrate new activities into your daily life.

3. Practice Self-Care: Prioritize self-care activities that promote relaxation and well-being. Engage in regular exercise, maintain a balanced diet, and prioritize sleep to ensure physical and mental health.

4. Explore New Opportunities: Transitioning to civilian life opens up a world of possibilities. Take time to explore different career paths, educational opportunities, or hobbies that align with your interests and goals. Embrace the chance to reinvent yourself and pursue new passions.

5. Communicate with Loved Ones: Open and honest communication with family, friends, and loved ones is crucial during this transition. Share your concerns, fears, and aspirations with them, and seek their understanding and support.

Conclusion:

The transition from military to civilian life can be overwhelming, but with proper stress management techniques, it can also be a time of growth and personal development. By understanding the challenges of this transition and implementing coping strategies, individuals can effectively navigate this period and successfully adapt to their new civilian life. Remember, seeking support, establishing routines, practicing self-care, exploring new opportunities, and maintaining open communication are key ingredients to managing stress during this transition.

Seeking Support from Veteran Organizations

For individuals who have served in the military, the transition back to civilian life can be a challenging and stressful process. The unique experiences and demands faced by veterans can often result in a range of emotional and psychological difficulties. However, there is a wealth of support available through veteran organizations that can provide assistance and guidance during this transitional period.

These veteran organizations are specifically designed to address the needs of former military personnel, offering a range of services tailored to support their mental, emotional, and physical well-being. One of the most significant benefits of seeking support from these organizations is the opportunity to connect with fellow veterans who have shared similar experiences. This sense of camaraderie can be invaluable in providing a safe space to share stories, exchange advice, and seek comfort from those who truly understand the challenges faced by veterans.

Veteran organizations often offer a variety of programs and resources aimed at helping veterans manage stress and improve their overall quality of life. These can include counseling services, support groups, wellness programs, and vocational training opportunities. Additionally, many veteran organizations provide assistance with navigating the complex systems of healthcare, education, and employment, ensuring that veterans have access to the resources they need to thrive in civilian life.

It is important to note that seeking support from veteran organizations is not limited to those struggling with mental health issues. Even if you feel that you are managing well, connecting with these organizations can still be incredibly beneficial. They can provide opportunities for personal and professional growth, as well as networking events and mentorship programs. By engaging with veteran organizations, you can continue to build a strong sense of community and connection with others who have served.

In conclusion, seeking support from veteran organizations is a crucial step in managing the stress and challenges associated with transitioning to civilian life. These organizations offer a wide range of resources and programs tailored to the unique needs of veterans, providing a supportive community and invaluable guidance. Whether you are struggling with mental health issues or simply looking to connect with others who have shared similar experiences, veteran organizations can be a lifeline in navigating the complexities of post-military life.

Addressing PTSD and Trauma-Related Stress

Post-Traumatic Stress Disorder (PTSD) and trauma-related stress can have a significant impact on individuals and their relationships. In this subchapter, we will explore the causes and symptoms of PTSD and trauma-related stress, as well as effective strategies for addressing and managing these challenges.

PTSD is a mental health condition that can develop after experiencing or witnessing a traumatic event. It affects individuals from all walks of life, including veterans, survivors of abuse or violence, and those who have been involved in accidents or natural disasters. Trauma-related stress, on the other hand, refers to the emotional and psychological effects of trauma, regardless of whether a person meets the criteria for a PTSD diagnosis.

Understanding the symptoms of PTSD and trauma-related stress is crucial for individuals and their loved ones. Common symptoms include intrusive thoughts or memories, nightmares, flashbacks, avoidance of triggers, hyperarousal, and changes in mood and cognition. It is important to note that these symptoms can vary from person to person, and seeking professional help is essential for accurate diagnosis and effective treatment.

For those experiencing PTSD or trauma-related stress, various strategies can help manage and alleviate symptoms. These may include therapy, such as cognitive-behavioral therapy (CBT) or eye movement desensitization and reprocessing (EMDR), medication, and self-care practices. Additionally, support from loved ones, creating a safe and nurturing environment, and engaging in stress reduction techniques like mindfulness and relaxation exercises can be beneficial.

This subchapter will also provide specific guidance for different niches, including workplace stress management, stress management for parents and caregivers, stress management for students and academics, stress management for entrepreneurs and business owners, stress management for athletes and sports professionals, stress management for healthcare professionals, stress management for veterans and military personnel, stress management for seniors and retirees, stress management for individuals with chronic illnesses or disabilities, and stress management for couples and relationships.

By understanding and addressing PTSD and trauma-related stress, individuals and their loved ones can cultivate healthier and more resilient relationships. This subchapter will serve as a valuable resource for anyone interested in understanding and managing these challenges, offering practical strategies and support for a wide range of audiences.

Note: The content provided in this subchapter is for informational purposes only and should not replace professional advice. It is recommended that individuals seek guidance from qualified mental health professionals for personalized assessment and treatment.

Strengthening Relationships after Military Service

Introduction:

Returning from military service can be a challenging and overwhelming experience for veterans and their loved ones. The transition from a highly structured and demanding environment to civilian life can lead to significant stress and strain on relationships. In this subchapter, we will explore effective strategies for strengthening relationships after military service. Whether you are a veteran, a spouse, a family member, or a friend, these insights will provide valuable guidance on how to navigate this unique and often difficult journey.

Understanding the Challenges:

The first step in strengthening relationships after military service is to acknowledge and understand the challenges that may arise. Veterans may experience physical and mental health issues, including post-traumatic stress disorder (PTSD), depression, or anxiety. These conditions can significantly impact their ability to communicate, connect, and adjust to civilian life. Spouses and family members may also face their own set of challenges, such as assuming new roles and responsibilities, dealing with changes in their loved one's behavior, or managing their own stress and anxiety.

Effective Communication:

Open and honest communication is essential in any relationship but becomes even more crucial when navigating the complexities of post-military life. Both veterans and their loved ones should be encouraged to express their feelings, concerns, and expectations openly while actively listening to each other. Effective communication can help foster empathy, understanding, and patience, creating a solid foundation for rebuilding trust and strengthening the relationship.

Seeking Support:

No one should face the challenges of post-military life alone. It is essential for veterans and their loved ones to seek support from various resources available to them. This may include professional counseling, support groups, community organizations, or online forums. Connecting with others who have shared similar experiences can provide a sense of belonging and understanding, helping to alleviate feelings of isolation and offering practical advice and guidance.

Establishing Routines:

Creating new routines and structure can help facilitate the transition from military to civilian life. By establishing regular schedules for activities, meals, and quality time together, veterans and their loved ones can regain a sense of stability and familiarity. Additionally, engaging in shared hobbies or activities can help strengthen the bond and create new positive experiences.

Patience and Understanding:

Above all, patience and understanding are critical when working to strengthen relationships after military service. Recognize that both veterans and their loved ones may need time to adjust and heal. Avoid placing unrealistic expectations on each other and instead focus on supporting one another through the ups and downs of the journey.

Conclusion:

Strengthening relationships after military service requires dedication, empathy, and effective communication. By understanding the challenges, seeking support, establishing routines, and practicing patience and understanding, veterans and their loved ones can navigate this transition with resilience and create stronger, more fulfilling relationships. Remember, you are not alone in this journey, and with the right tools and support, you can build a love that withstands the pressures of post-military life.

Chapter 9: Stress Management for Seniors and Retirees

Adjusting to Retirement and Coping with Change

Retirement is a significant life transition that can bring about a mix of emotions and challenges. After spending years in the workforce, it is natural to feel a sense of loss, a shift in identity, and uncertainty about what lies ahead. However, with the right mindset and tools, adjusting to retirement and coping with change can be a fulfilling and exciting chapter in your life.

In this subchapter, we will explore the unique stressors and opportunities that retirement brings. Whether you are a retiree or someone supporting a retiree, understanding and managing stress during this transition is crucial for maintaining well-being and healthy relationships.

For retirees, it is essential to recognize that retirement is not an endpoint but a new beginning. It is an opportunity to rediscover yourself, pursue new interests, and create a meaningful and fulfilling life. However, it is common to face challenges such as financial concerns, a loss of social connections, and a lack of structure. We will provide practical strategies for managing these stressors, including financial planning, building new social networks, and establishing a daily routine that brings purpose and joy.

Additionally, we will address the impact of retirement on relationships, particularly for couples. The shift in dynamics and increased time spent together can be both rewarding and challenging. We will explore effective communication strategies, ways to nurture intimacy, and how to maintain a healthy balance between individuality and togetherness.

This subchapter will also provide insights into coping with change for different niches. Whether you are a student, healthcare professional, entrepreneur, or veteran, retirement brings a unique set of stressors and adjustments. We will offer tailored strategies for managing stress during this transition, taking into account the specific needs and challenges of each niche.

Understanding and managing stress during retirement is not only important for individuals but also for their families and caregivers. We will provide guidance for loved ones on how to support and adapt to the retiree's changing needs, ensuring a smooth transition and strong support system.

In conclusion, adjusting to retirement and coping with change can be a transformative and rewarding experience. By embracing the opportunities that retirement brings and implementing effective stress management strategies, retirees can navigate this transition with grace and joy. This subchapter aims to provide valuable insights and practical tools to help individuals and their loved ones thrive during this new chapter of life.

Maintaining Mental and Physical Well-Being in Older Age

As we age, it becomes increasingly important to prioritize our mental and physical well-being. In older age, we may face unique challenges, such as chronic illnesses, disabilities, or the loss of loved ones. However, by adopting certain strategies and making conscious choices, we can continue to lead fulfilling and healthy lives. In this subchapter, we will explore various techniques and tips on how to maintain mental and physical well-being in older age.

1. Engage in regular physical activity: Physical activity is crucial for maintaining a healthy body and mind. Engaging in regular exercise, such as walking, swimming, or yoga, can help improve cardiovascular

health, strengthen muscles, and reduce the risk of chronic conditions like diabetes and arthritis. It also releases endorphins, which are natural mood boosters.

2. Prioritize mental stimulation: Keeping your mind active is just as important as staying physically active. Engage in activities that challenge your brain, such as puzzles, reading, learning a new language, or playing musical instruments. These activities can help improve memory, cognitive function, and overall mental well-being.

3. Maintain a balanced diet: Eating a nutritious and well-balanced diet is essential for overall health and well-being. Include a variety of fruits, vegetables, whole grains, lean proteins, and healthy fats in your meals. Limit the consumption of processed foods, sugary snacks, and excessive salt or caffeine.

4. Stay socially active: Maintaining social connections is vital for mental and emotional well-being. Join community groups, clubs, or volunteer organizations that align with your interests. Regularly connect with friends, family, and loved ones to combat feelings of loneliness or isolation.

5. Prioritize self-care: Take time for yourself and engage in activities that bring you joy and relaxation. This could include hobbies, meditation, practicing mindfulness, or simply taking a walk in nature. Prioritizing self-care allows you to recharge and reduce stress levels.

6. Regular health check-ups: Schedule regular visits with healthcare professionals to monitor your physical health and address any concerns promptly. It is crucial to stay on top of preventive screenings, vaccinations, and managing chronic conditions effectively.

By incorporating these strategies into your daily routine, you can maintain optimal mental and physical well-being in older age.

Remember, it's never too late to start prioritizing your health and taking steps towards a happier and healthier life.

This subchapter is a valuable resource for individuals of all backgrounds and professions, including understanding and managing stress, workplace stress management, stress management for parents and caregivers, stress management for students and academics, stress management for entrepreneurs and business owners, stress management for athletes and sports professionals, stress management for healthcare professionals, stress management for veterans and military personnel, stress management for seniors and retirees, stress management for individuals with chronic illnesses or disabilities, and stress management for couples and relationships.

Social Support and Engagement for Seniors

As we age, it becomes increasingly important to prioritize our mental and emotional well-being. One crucial aspect of this is maintaining social support and engagement. In this subchapter, we will explore the significance of social connections for seniors and provide practical strategies to enhance social support, combat isolation, and foster a sense of belonging.

Research consistently shows that social isolation can have detrimental effects on seniors' physical and mental health. Loneliness has been linked to an increased risk of developing chronic illnesses, depression, and cognitive decline. Therefore, it is crucial for seniors to actively seek and maintain social connections.

One effective way to combat social isolation is by engaging in social activities. Seniors can join local clubs or organizations that align with their interests, such as book clubs, gardening groups, or volunteer organizations. These activities not only provide an opportunity to connect with like-minded individuals but also offer a sense of purpose and fulfillment.

Technology has also become a valuable tool for seniors to stay connected with friends and family. Social media platforms allow them to keep in touch, share experiences, and participate in online communities. Additionally, there are numerous online platforms specifically designed for seniors to meet new people and engage in virtual activities, such as online classes, games, and discussion forums.

Furthermore, fostering intergenerational connections can be immensely beneficial for both seniors and younger individuals. Seniors can offer wisdom, guidance, and a unique perspective, while younger generations can provide companionship, energy, and technological assistance. Volunteering at schools, mentoring programs, or intergenerational housing initiatives are excellent ways to bridge the generation gap and create mutually beneficial relationships.

Lastly, community-based support programs can provide seniors with a network of resources and assistance. These programs may offer transportation services, meal delivery, or social events specifically tailored for seniors. Additionally, support groups can provide a safe space for seniors to share their experiences, receive emotional support, and learn coping strategies from others who are facing similar challenges.

In conclusion, social support and engagement are vital for seniors' overall well-being. By actively seeking social connections, engaging in social activities, utilizing technology, fostering intergenerational relationships, and accessing community-based support programs, seniors can combat social isolation and enhance their quality of life. Remember, it is never too late to build new friendships, explore new interests, and create a supportive network that will contribute to a fulfilling and happy life in the golden years.

Managing Stressful Life Events in Later Years

As we age, we often face numerous challenges and stressful life events that can significantly impact our overall well-being. Whether it's dealing with retirement, loss of loved ones, declining health, or financial concerns, these stressors can take a toll on our mental and physical health. In this subchapter, we will explore effective strategies for managing stressful life events in later years, providing valuable insights and techniques to help individuals navigate these difficult times.

Retirement is a significant life transition that can bring both excitement and anxiety. Many individuals may feel a loss of purpose or struggle with the sudden change in routine. It's crucial to approach retirement with a positive mindset and create a new sense of purpose. Engaging in meaningful activities, such as volunteering, pursuing hobbies, or starting a new business venture, can help fill the void and provide a sense of fulfillment.

Loss of loved ones is another common stressor in later years. Grief can be overwhelming, and it's important to give yourself permission to mourn and seek support from loved ones or support groups. Embracing self-care activities, such as exercise, meditation, or therapy, can also help individuals cope with the pain and find solace in the healing process.

Declining health can be a significant stressor for seniors, but there are various strategies to manage and improve overall well-being. Staying physically active, eating a balanced diet, and maintaining regular medical check-ups are essential for maintaining good health. Additionally, adopting stress-reducing practices, such as mindfulness and relaxation techniques, can help individuals cope with health-related challenges and improve their quality of life.

Financial concerns can also be a significant stressor in later years, particularly for retirees. Creating a realistic budget, seeking financial advice, and exploring additional sources of income can alleviate some of the financial stress. Moreover, building a support network and engaging in social activities can provide emotional support and reduce feelings of isolation.

In conclusion, managing stressful life events in later years requires a proactive approach and the adoption of various coping strategies. By embracing a positive mindset, seeking support from loved ones, engaging in self-care activities, and exploring new opportunities, individuals can navigate these challenges and maintain their overall well-being. Remember, it's never too late to start anew and prioritize your mental and physical health.

Enhancing Relationships in the Golden Years

As we age, our relationships often take on a new significance and importance. The golden years are a time for reflection, growth, and cherishing the bonds we have built over a lifetime. However, this stage of life can also bring its fair share of stress and challenges. In this subchapter, we will explore strategies for enhancing relationships in the golden years, providing guidance and support for individuals and couples alike.

Stress can manifest in various ways during the golden years, whether it's due to retirement, health concerns, or changes in roles and responsibilities. Understanding and managing stress is crucial for maintaining healthy relationships. We will delve into effective stress management techniques, such as mindfulness, relaxation exercises, and communication skills, that can help individuals and couples navigate these challenges together.

Workplace stress management is an important aspect for those still engaged in the workforce during their golden years. We will discuss strategies for finding a healthy work-life balance, setting boundaries, and managing the pressures of the workplace. By implementing these techniques, individuals can mitigate stress and cultivate a more harmonious relationship with their work and their partners.

For parents and caregivers in the golden years, stress management becomes even more critical. The demands of caring for children or aging parents can take a toll on relationships. We will explore ways to create support networks, establish self-care routines, and communicate effectively with loved ones during these demanding times.

Students and academics may also face unique stressors during the golden years, such as returning to school or pursuing lifelong learning. We will address strategies for time management, maintaining focus, and managing the pressures of academic life. These tools will aid in fostering stronger relationships both within the academic community and with partners.

Entrepreneurs and business owners in their golden years may experience stress related to managing a business or transitioning into retirement. We will provide insights on delegating tasks, setting realistic goals, and maintaining a healthy work-life balance. These strategies will not only enhance relationships with partners but also help entrepreneurs navigate this new chapter of life.

Other niches, such as athletes, healthcare professionals, veterans, individuals with chronic illnesses or disabilities, and retirees, will find valuable guidance on managing stress and enhancing relationships in the golden years. We will explore tailored techniques for each group, taking into account their unique circumstances and challenges.

In conclusion, the golden years provide an opportunity for individuals and couples to strengthen their relationships and find fulfillment. By understanding and managing stress, setting boundaries, and cultivating effective communication skills, individuals can navigate this stage of life with grace and create lasting connections with their loved ones. This subchapter will serve as a comprehensive guide for anyone looking to enhance their relationships in the golden years.

Chapter 10: Stress Management for Individuals with Chronic Illnesses or Disabilities

Understanding the Impact of Chronic Illness and Disability on Stress

Living with a chronic illness or disability can have a profound impact on a person's stress levels and overall well-being. In this subchapter, we will explore the various ways in which chronic illness and disability can influence stress and provide strategies for effectively managing it.

Chronic illness and disability often bring about a range of physical, emotional, and psychological challenges. The daily demands of managing symptoms, frequent medical appointments, and limitations on activities can lead to feelings of frustration, anxiety, and helplessness. Additionally, individuals may experience social isolation, financial burdens, and a loss of independence, further exacerbating stress levels.

For individuals in the workforce, managing a chronic illness or disability can present unique challenges. Workplace stress management becomes crucial as individuals navigate the need for accommodations, discrimination, and the fear of job loss. We will delve into strategies for advocating for oneself, creating a supportive work environment, and finding a balance between work and self-care.

Parents and caregivers of individuals with chronic illness or disability face their own set of stressors. Juggling the responsibilities of caregiving, managing medical appointments, and ensuring the well-being of their loved ones can be overwhelming. We will discuss effective stress management techniques, including self-care, seeking support from others, and setting realistic expectations.

For students and academics, the pressure to excel academically while managing a chronic illness or disability can be incredibly challenging. We will explore strategies for time management, seeking accommodations, and cultivating a support network to alleviate stress and promote academic success.

Entrepreneurs and business owners with chronic illnesses or disabilities face unique stressors related to managing their own businesses. We will provide insights into effective stress management techniques, including delegation, time management, and prioritization.

Athletes and sports professionals may also experience the impact of chronic illness or disability on their performance and overall well-being. We will discuss strategies for self-care, adaptive training techniques, and seeking support from coaches and teammates.

Healthcare professionals, veterans, military personnel, seniors, and individuals with chronic illnesses or disabilities all have their own specific stressors and challenges. We will provide tailored strategies for each group, recognizing the unique circumstances they face and providing practical tools for stress management.

Finally, we will explore stress management within relationships. Chronic illness or disability can place strain on partnerships, and we will discuss effective communication, empathy, and self-care techniques to maintain healthy relationships.

By understanding the impact of chronic illness and disability on stress, individuals can develop effective strategies to manage their stress levels and improve their overall well-being. Whether you are a caregiver, student, athlete, or healthcare professional, this subchapter will provide valuable insights and tools for successfully navigating the challenges associated with chronic illness and disability.

Building Resilience and Coping with Daily Challenges

In today's fast-paced and demanding world, stress has become an integral part of our daily lives. It affects not only individuals but also couples and relationships. The ability to build resilience and effectively cope with these challenges is crucial for maintaining a healthy and thriving life. This subchapter aims to provide practical strategies and techniques for understanding and managing stress in various areas of life.

Understanding and Managing Stress:

Stress is a natural response to the demands and pressures we face in our personal and professional lives. Understanding the triggers and effects of stress is the first step towards managing it effectively. By recognizing the signs of stress, individuals can take proactive steps to reduce its impact and prevent it from escalating into more severe issues like anxiety or depression.

Workplace Stress Management:

The modern workplace is often a hotbed for stress. Long hours, tight deadlines, and interpersonal conflicts can all contribute to an overwhelming work environment. This section will focus on techniques for managing workplace stress, including time management, setting boundaries, and practicing self-care.

Stress Management for Parents and Caregivers:

Parenting and caregiving come with their unique set of stressors. Juggling multiple responsibilities, lack of sleep, and constant worry can take a toll on one's well-being. This section will offer strategies for self-care, communication, and finding support networks to help parents and caregivers better cope with their daily challenges.

Stress Management for Students and Academics:

The academic world can be highly demanding, placing significant pressure on students and academics. This subchapter will provide practical tips for managing study-related stress, time management, and building healthy study habits. It will also explore techniques for maintaining work-life balance and finding support within the academic community.

Stress Management for Entrepreneurs and Business Owners:

Entrepreneurs and business owners face unique stressors related to running their own ventures. Balancing financial pressures, decision-making, and maintaining work-life harmony can be overwhelming. This section will offer strategies for effective stress management, including delegation, goal-setting, and self-reflection.

Stress Management for Athletes and Sports Professionals:

Athletes and sports professionals often experience stress from intense competition, training demands, and performance expectations. This subchapter will explore techniques for managing stress in sports, including mindfulness, visualization, and building a strong support system.

Stress Management for Healthcare Professionals:

Healthcare professionals are at the forefront of dealing with stress on a daily basis. This section will address the challenges faced by doctors, nurses, and other healthcare providers and offer strategies for self-care, emotional resilience, and communication in high-pressure environments.

Stress Management for Veterans and Military Personnel:

Military personnel and veterans often experience unique stressors related to their service. This subchapter will focus on coping mechanisms and resources available to help them manage stress, including therapy, peer support, and mindfulness practices.

Stress Management for Seniors and Retirees:

Even in later stages of life, stress can still be a significant factor. This section will explore strategies for seniors and retirees to maintain emotional well-being, adapt to life changes, and find purpose and fulfillment in their daily lives.

Stress Management for Individuals with Chronic Illnesses or Disabilities:

Living with chronic illnesses or disabilities can be physically and emotionally challenging. This subchapter will provide guidance on managing stress related to health conditions, including self-care practices, support systems, and adaptive coping strategies.

Stress Management for Couples and Relationships:

Stress can take a toll on relationships, leading to conflict, communication breakdown, and emotional distance. This section will offer practical advice on how couples can support each other through stressful times, enhance communication, and strengthen their bond.

In conclusion, building resilience and effectively coping with daily challenges is essential for maintaining a healthy and thriving life. This subchapter will provide valuable insights and strategies for understanding and managing stress in various areas of life, catering to a wide range of audiences, including individuals, couples, and specialized niches. By implementing these techniques, individuals can enhance their well-being and forge stronger relationships in the face of stress.

Seeking Support from Healthcare Providers and Support Groups

In times of stress and pressure, seeking support from healthcare providers and support groups can be a game-changer. In this subchapter, we will explore the importance of reaching out for help, the benefits of healthcare professionals, and the power of support groups in managing stress and improving relationships.

When stress becomes overwhelming, it is crucial to recognize that seeking support is not a sign of weakness, but rather a strength. Healthcare providers, including therapists, counselors, and psychologists, are trained professionals who can offer guidance, tools, and strategies to help individuals and couples navigate stress effectively. They can provide a safe space to discuss concerns, offer coping mechanisms, and help develop personalized stress management plans.

For those facing workplace stress, healthcare providers can guide individuals in creating a work-life balance, setting boundaries, and managing expectations. They can also assist in developing resilience skills, communication techniques, and conflict resolution strategies that can significantly improve relationships within the workplace.

Parents and caregivers often face unique stressors, and seeking support from healthcare professionals can be invaluable. They can help parents develop effective parenting techniques, manage time and responsibilities, and address any challenges that arise. Additionally, joining support groups specifically tailored for parents and caregivers can provide a sense of community, shared experiences, and practical advice.

Students and academics, entrepreneurs and business owners, athletes and sports professionals, veterans and military personnel, seniors and retirees, and individuals with chronic illnesses or disabilities all have their own set of stressors. Healthcare providers can offer tailored support to address their specific needs and challenges. They can provide guidance on time management, self-care, stress reduction techniques, and resilience-building strategies.

Support groups, whether in-person or online, are another powerful resource for stress management. These groups offer a sense of belonging, understanding, and empathy. Sharing experiences and learning from others who have faced similar challenges can be incredibly empowering and validating. Support groups also provide an opportunity to exchange coping strategies, gain insights, and build a network of support.

In conclusion, seeking support from healthcare providers and joining support groups can greatly enhance stress management and improve relationships. Whether you are an individual facing stress or a couple navigating relationship challenges, reaching out for help is a courageous step towards a healthier and happier life. Remember, you are not alone, and there are professionals and support groups ready to assist you on your stress management journey.

Self-Care Techniques for Managing Stress and Symptoms

In today's fast-paced and demanding world, stress has become an everyday part of our lives. Whether you are a working professional, a parent, a student, an entrepreneur, a healthcare professional, a veteran, or someone with a chronic illness or disability, stress can have a profound impact on your well-being and relationships. However, there are effective self-care techniques that can help you manage stress and its symptoms, allowing you to lead a more balanced and fulfilling life.

Understanding and managing stress is the key to overcoming its negative effects. One important technique is practicing mindfulness and relaxation exercises. This involves taking time out of your day to focus on the present moment, letting go of worries and anxieties. Deep breathing exercises, meditation, and yoga can all help you achieve a state of calm and reduce stress levels.

For workplace stress management, it is crucial to set boundaries and prioritize self-care. Learn to say no when you are overwhelmed, delegate tasks, and take regular breaks. Engaging in physical activities such as walking, jogging, or dancing can also help release tension and boost your mood.

Parents and caregivers often experience high levels of stress due to the demands of their roles. It is important to schedule time for self-care, whether it's going for a walk, reading a book, or engaging in a hobby. Seeking support from other parents or joining a support group can also provide a valuable network for sharing experiences and coping strategies.

Students and academics face unique stressors related to academic performance and deadlines. Time management, setting realistic goals, and maintaining a healthy work-life balance are essential for managing stress. Prioritize self-care activities like exercise, socializing, and relaxation to recharge your mind and body.

Entrepreneurs and business owners often face immense pressure and uncertainty. Developing a self-care routine that includes regular exercise, healthy eating, and sleep is crucial for managing stress and preventing burnout. Additionally, seeking support from mentors or joining entrepreneurial communities can provide valuable guidance and understanding.

Stress management for athletes and sports professionals involves a holistic approach that includes physical, mental, and emotional well-being. Practicing mindfulness, engaging in relaxation techniques, and ensuring adequate rest and recovery are essential for optimal performance and stress reduction.

Healthcare professionals, veterans, and military personnel frequently experience high levels of stress due to the demanding nature of their work. It is important to practice self-compassion, seek support from colleagues, and engage in stress-reducing activities such as exercise and hobbies to maintain overall well-being.

Seniors, retirees, and individuals with chronic illnesses or disabilities require special attention to manage stress. Engaging in activities that promote physical and mental well-being, such as gentle exercise, socializing, and engaging in hobbies or creative outlets, can help reduce stress and improve overall quality of life.

Finally, stress management for couples and relationships is crucial for maintaining healthy connections. Engaging in shared activities, practicing effective communication, and prioritizing quality time together can help reduce stress and strengthen the bond between partners.

In conclusion, managing stress and its symptoms is essential for leading a balanced and fulfilling life. By understanding the unique stressors faced by different individuals and implementing self-care techniques, you can effectively manage stress and improve your overall well-being and relationships. Remember, self-care is not selfish, it is a necessary component of a healthy and thriving life.

Nurturing Healthy Relationships and Seeking Understanding

In today's fast-paced and demanding world, stress has become a constant companion for many of us. The pressure to excel at work, meet family expectations, and juggle various responsibilities can take a toll on our relationships. However, it is essential to recognize that stress management is not just an individual endeavor but also a crucial aspect of maintaining healthy relationships.

Understanding and Managing Stress:

Stress affects every aspect of our lives, including our relationships. By understanding the impact of stress on ourselves and our loved ones, we can better manage its effects. This subchapter will explore the various ways stress can manifest in relationships and provide practical strategies for identifying and addressing stressors effectively.

Workplace Stress Management:

Work-related stress can significantly strain relationships, as the demands of the job often spill over into personal life. This section will offer guidance on how to navigate workplace stress, set boundaries, and create a healthy work-life balance to protect and nurture relationships.

Stress Management for Parents and Caregivers:

Parenting and caregiving can be incredibly rewarding but also incredibly stressful. This subchapter will delve into the unique challenges faced by parents and caregivers, providing tips on managing stress, fostering open communication, and finding support networks to strengthen relationships in the face of adversity.

Stress Management for Students and Academics:

Students and academics face intense pressure to perform academically and professionally. This section will provide practical tools to help students and academics manage stress, maintain healthy relationships, and prioritize self-care amidst demanding schedules and high expectations.

Stress Management for Entrepreneurs and Business Owners:

Entrepreneurs and business owners often grapple with the weight of responsibility and the constant pressure to succeed. This subchapter will offer strategies to navigate the unique stressors faced by entrepreneurs, while preserving and nurturing their personal relationships.

Stress Management for Athletes and Sports Professionals:

Competitive sports can be a significant source of stress for athletes and sports professionals. This section will explore techniques to manage performance-related stress, enhance communication within relationships, and strike a balance between demanding training schedules and personal connections.

Stress Management for Healthcare Professionals:

Healthcare professionals work in high-pressure environments, which can impact their well-being and relationships. This subchapter will address the unique stressors faced by healthcare professionals, providing insights on managing stress, fostering emotional support, and maintaining healthy relationships.

Stress Management for Veterans and Military Personnel:

Veterans and military personnel often experience trauma and high levels of stress. This section will explore strategies to cope with post-traumatic stress, reconnect with loved ones, and rebuild relationships strained by military service.

Stress Management for Seniors and Retirees:

As we age, stress can take different forms. This subchapter will focus on managing stress in retirement, maintaining social connections, and nurturing relationships to ensure a fulfilling and satisfying later life.

Stress Management for Individuals with Chronic Illnesses or Disabilities:

Living with chronic illnesses or disabilities can be emotionally and physically draining. This section will provide guidance on managing stress, seeking support, and fostering relationships that endure through challenging times.

Stress Management for Couples and Relationships:

Finally, this subchapter will explore how stress impacts romantic relationships, providing tools for effective communication, conflict resolution, and mutual support. It will emphasize the importance of nurturing relationships amidst stress and offer practical suggestions for building resilience as a couple.

In "Love Under Pressure: Stress Management for Couples and Relationships in the Modern World," readers from various walks of life will find valuable insights and practical strategies to nurture healthy relationships and seek understanding amidst the pressures of the modern world. Whether you are a stressed-out student, a time-pressed entrepreneur, or a healthcare professional dealing with immense responsibilities, this book will guide you towards building stronger connections while managing stress effectively.

Chapter 11: Stress Management for Couples and Relationships

Communication Strategies for Stressful Times

In today's fast-paced and demanding world, it's no surprise that stress has become a common aspect of our lives. Whether you are a parent, a student, an athlete, a healthcare professional, or simply someone trying to navigate through a challenging relationship, stress can weigh heavily on your well-being. However, there is hope. By implementing effective communication strategies during these stressful times, you can not only alleviate stress but also strengthen your relationships and improve your overall quality of life.

One of the key elements in managing stress is open and honest communication. By expressing your feelings, concerns, and needs to the people around you, you can create a supportive network that understands and empathizes with your struggles. This is especially important in the workplace, where stress can often be magnified due to high expectations and deadlines. Communicating with your colleagues and superiors about your workload, setting realistic goals, and seeking assistance when needed can help alleviate workplace stress and foster a healthier work environment.

For parents and caregivers, communicating with your children is vital in helping them understand and manage their own stress. By creating a safe space for open dialogue, you can teach them effective coping mechanisms, encourage healthy expression of emotions, and strengthen the bond between you and your child. Similarly, students and academics can benefit from effective communication strategies by seeking support from their peers and professors, setting clear boundaries, and expressing their needs for a balanced academic and personal life.

Entrepreneurs and business owners often face immense stress as they navigate the challenges of running a business. By fostering a culture of open communication within their teams, setting realistic expectations, and encouraging regular feedback, they can create a supportive and collaborative working environment that minimizes stress and maximizes productivity.

Stress management is also crucial for athletes and sports professionals, as the pressure to perform can often be overwhelming. Effective communication with coaches, teammates, and support staff can help athletes express their concerns, discuss their goals, and seek assistance when needed, ultimately enhancing their performance and well-being.

Healthcare professionals, veterans, seniors, and individuals with chronic illnesses or disabilities all face unique stressors in their lives. By establishing open lines of communication with their healthcare providers, support groups, and loved ones, they can better manage their stress, seek appropriate help, and find comfort in knowing they are not alone.

Lastly, communication strategies play a vital role in maintaining healthy relationships. By expressing your needs, concerns, and emotions to your partner, family members, or friends, you can build a stronger support system that can weather the storms of stress together.

In conclusion, effective communication strategies are essential for managing stress in various aspects of life. By fostering open and honest dialogue, seeking support, and expressing your needs, you can alleviate stress, strengthen relationships, and improve your overall well-being. Remember, you are not alone in your struggles, and by reaching out, you can find the support and guidance you need to navigate through even the most stressful times.

Mutual Support and Understanding in Relationships

In today's fast-paced and demanding world, stress has become an inevitable part of our lives. It affects not only individuals but also their relationships, be it with their partners, family, friends, or colleagues. Managing stress becomes crucial for maintaining healthy and fulfilling relationships. In this subchapter, we will explore the significance of mutual support and understanding in relationships as a powerful tool for stress management.

Stress can create rifts and misunderstandings in even the strongest of relationships. It is essential to recognize that both partners may be experiencing stress from various sources, such as work, parenting, or personal challenges. By acknowledging and empathizing with each other's stress, couples can create an environment of mutual support.

Communication is key when it comes to understanding and managing stress in relationships. It is important to openly express your concerns, fears, and anxieties to your partner. By doing so, you create an opportunity for them to provide the support you need. Active listening and showing empathy towards your partner's stress will help them feel understood and validated. This mutual understanding can strengthen the bond between partners and alleviate stress levels.

In addition to effective communication, couples can also engage in stress management activities together. This could include meditation, yoga, or engaging in hobbies that bring joy and relaxation. By sharing these experiences, couples can not only support each other but also find a space to unwind and rejuvenate together.

It is equally important to recognize that stress affects individuals differently. In relationships where one partner is facing higher stress levels, the other partner can offer additional support and understanding. Being aware of each other's triggers and stressors can help prevent unnecessary conflicts and promote a more harmonious relationship.

Furthermore, seeking external support, such as counseling or therapy, can be immensely beneficial for couples dealing with high levels of stress. A professional can guide them in developing effective coping strategies, improving communication, and fostering a stronger bond.

In conclusion, mutual support and understanding are vital in managing stress within relationships. By actively listening, empathizing, and engaging in stress management activities together, couples can nurture a healthier and more resilient bond. Remember, stress is an unavoidable part of life, but with mutual support, it can be effectively managed, allowing couples to thrive even in the face of adversity.

Balancing Individual and Relationship Needs

In today's modern world, where stress seems to be an inevitable part of our daily lives, it is crucial to find ways to manage and alleviate the pressures that can impact our relationships. Love Under Pressure: Stress Management for Couples and Relationships in the Modern World provides valuable insights and strategies on how to achieve a harmonious balance between individual and relationship needs.

Understanding and managing stress is a universal concern that affects people from all walks of life. Whether you are a professional dealing with workplace stress, a parent juggling multiple responsibilities, a student pursuing academic success, an entrepreneur striving for business growth, an athlete pushing yourself to excel, a healthcare professional caring for others, a veteran or military personnel coping with the aftermath of service, a senior or retiree navigating life's challenges, or an individual with chronic illnesses or disabilities, stress management is essential for your overall well-being.

This subchapter delves into the delicate balance between individual and relationship needs in the context of stress management. It explores how stress can impact both partners in a relationship and provides guidance on how to effectively navigate these challenges.

For couples, it is important to recognize and acknowledge each other's individual needs while also nurturing the needs of the relationship itself. This involves open communication, empathy, and a willingness to compromise. By understanding and supporting each other's stress management strategies, couples can create an environment of mutual understanding and respect.

The subchapter also emphasizes the significance of self-care in maintaining a healthy relationship. Taking care of oneself is not selfish; it is a vital component of being able to show up fully in a relationship. It offers practical tips and techniques for self-care, such as engaging in regular exercise, practicing mindfulness and relaxation techniques, and seeking support from friends, family, or professionals.

Furthermore, it explores the importance of setting boundaries and managing expectations within a relationship. This includes discussions around work-life balance, prioritizing quality time together, and finding ways to support each other's personal goals and passions.

In conclusion, balancing individual and relationship needs is a fundamental aspect of stress management for couples and relationships. Love Under Pressure offers valuable insights and practical strategies for the public, encompassing various niches such as workplace stress management, stress management for parents and caregivers, stress management for students and academics, stress management for entrepreneurs and business owners, stress management for athletes and sports professionals, stress management for healthcare professionals, stress management for veterans and military personnel, stress management for seniors and retirees, and stress management for individuals with chronic illnesses or disabilities. By finding this delicate equilibrium, couples can navigate the challenges of stress together, strengthening their bond and fostering a healthier, more fulfilling relationship.

Developing Healthy Coping Mechanisms as a Couple

In today's fast-paced and demanding world, stress has become an inevitable part of our lives. It affects not only individuals but also couples and relationships. The ability to cope with stress is crucial for maintaining a healthy and thriving partnership. In this subchapter, we will explore effective strategies and techniques that couples can use to develop healthy coping mechanisms and strengthen their bond in the face of stress.

Stress can manifest in various forms, from work-related challenges to parenting responsibilities, academic pressures, or health issues. Regardless of the specific source, stress impacts both partners and can strain the relationship if not managed effectively. However, by working together and employing healthy coping mechanisms, couples can navigate these challenges and emerge stronger than ever.

One of the most important aspects of developing healthy coping mechanisms as a couple is open and honest communication. It is essential to create a safe space where both partners can express their feelings and concerns without fear of judgment or reprisal. By actively listening to each other and providing support, couples can better understand and empathize with their partner's stressors.

Another crucial aspect is self-care. It is vital for couples to prioritize their own well-being in order to effectively support each other. This may include engaging in regular exercise, practicing mindfulness or meditation, pursuing hobbies or interests, and maintaining a healthy work-life balance. By taking care of themselves, couples can better manage stress and be more present and supportive to their partner.

Additionally, couples can explore various stress management techniques together. These may include deep breathing exercises, relaxation techniques, or engaging in activities that promote stress reduction, such as yoga or nature walks. By engaging in shared stress-reducing activities, couples can bond and create a positive and supportive environment.

Lastly, seeking professional help should not be overlooked. Couples can benefit from couples therapy or counseling, where they can learn additional coping strategies and gain perspective from an unbiased third party. A therapist can guide couples in identifying and addressing the root causes of stress within their relationship and provide effective tools for managing it.

In conclusion, developing healthy coping mechanisms as a couple is crucial for navigating the stresses of modern life. By fostering open communication, prioritizing self-care, exploring stress management techniques together, and seeking professional help when needed, couples can build resilience and strengthen their relationship. Remember, stress is inevitable, but the way we handle it can make all the difference.

Strengthening the Relationship through Stress Management

In today's fast-paced and demanding world, stress has become an inevitable part of our lives. It affects every aspect of our existence, including our relationships. Whether you are a couple trying to navigate the challenges of daily life or an individual dealing with the pressures of work, parenting, caregiving, or any other role, stress can take a toll on your relationship.

"Love Under Pressure: Stress Management for Couples and Relationships in the Modern World" is a comprehensive guide that addresses the unique stressors faced by different individuals and provides practical strategies to strengthen relationships through stress management. This subchapter focuses on how stress impacts relationships and offers valuable insights for various niches.

Understanding and Managing Stress is the first step towards building resilience in relationships. This section delves into the science behind stress and its effects on our mind, body, and emotions. By understanding the physiological and psychological aspects of stress, individuals can develop better coping mechanisms and communicate their needs effectively.

Workplace stress management is a crucial topic in today's professional world, where career demands often spill over into personal lives. This subchapter explores strategies to balance work and personal life, set boundaries, and manage stressors unique to the workplace. It provides tools for couples to support each other in navigating work-related challenges and preventing burnout.

For parents and caregivers, stress management becomes even more critical as they juggle multiple responsibilities. This section offers practical tips to maintain a healthy work-life balance, manage parental stress, and nurture the couple's relationship amidst the demands of caregiving.

Students and academics face their own set of stressors, from academic pressure to deadlines and competition. This subchapter provides effective stress management techniques, such as time management, self-care, and seeking support, to help students and academics maintain healthy relationships while pursuing their goals.

Entrepreneurs and business owners often bear the weight of their ventures on their shoulders, which can strain relationships. This section offers strategies to manage stress in high-pressure environments, foster effective communication, and create a supportive partnership that withstands the challenges of entrepreneurship.

Stress management is also crucial for athletes, sports professionals, healthcare professionals, veterans, seniors, individuals with chronic illnesses or disabilities, and any individual in a relationship. This subchapter acknowledges the unique stressors faced by these niches and provides tailored strategies to strengthen relationships through stress management.

www.ingramcontent.com/pod-product-compliance
Lightning Source LLC
Chambersburg PA
CBHW021956170726
47994CB00021B/720